Before I

Making necessary change
to enjoy your jubilee

RUTH MATEOLA

RM
PUBLICATIONS

BEFORE I TURN 50

Ruth Mateola

Published by
Ruth Mateola Publications
An imprint of The Hadassah Network

41 Blundells Road,
Bradville, Milton Keynes
MK13 7HD
United Kingdom

Email: info@hadassahnetwork.com
Website: www.hadassahnetwork.com

First published 2021

ISBN 978-1-9996513-1-2

Cover Design / book layout: Imaginovation Ltd.

Printed in the United Kingdom.

Contents

"You can't reach your potential by remaining in a past due season. Your breakthrough is coming. Strongholds are breaking. Get Ready!"

- Germany Kent

Introduction

AT A cousin's 50th and wedding renewal party three years
ago, in the beautiful ancient city of Malta where we
had arrived to celebrate this awesome milestone with my
cousin, the Friday night started off with a get together at a
local club. My husband and I really did not want to be in that
atmosphere of a night club with all the smoking, dancing and
drinking, but for the sake of family, we braced ourselves and
went anyway.

There were at least 100 of us that came from London, all
of different age groups—some were older than 50, some in
their 40s, at the tip of turning 50. As soon as people arrived,
they immediately started indulging in alcohol consumption,
meaningless jesting, dancing and all sorts. I sat there, stunned
by what I was seeing. It was as if I left the room and was in
my own world and all I could think of was, wow! Is this what
turning 50 means?

What have these people achieved that makes them feel
they can still be partying and, in my opinion, wasting hard
earned money on alcohol to the point where the celebrant

and some friends left the venue drunk? Is this what celebrating 50 all about?

This experience was where the whole journey of this book began and I started to ask myself some tough questions which I am hoping you will ask yourself, and find the right answers so you can do some tangible things with your life before you celebrate the big 50.

You see, 50 is such a significant milestone of life that you must be prepared specially for it. I'm not saying you don't prepare for other significant years but 50 is a crossroad point that really defines the rest of your life because in our world today, many don't make it to that age, so if God allows you to make it, you owe it to God and yourself to prepare for that season of your life.

I realised that night that I have only seen three categories of people in my journey of life; those who manage life, those who waste life and those who thrive in life. Unfortunately, many fall in one of the first two categories and by the time they turn 50, rather than have a better plan for the rest of the journey, they just resort into doing the same things they have always done. They have no plans for change.

I am writing this book not as an expert but as someone burdened for a generation that has not done too well. I was 48 years old when I attended that birthday party and I left that weekend greatly challenged my own status quo, but determining to answer some key questions for myself and prepare well for this great season that will soon manifest in my life that I am now excited about.

I hope as you read this book, you too will be challenged but encouraged with great determination to recognise that your life is not a dress rehearsal but the real event, and you will make great preparation regardless of daily circumstances to make sure that there will be more to you and the life you have lived and still want to live before you turn 50.

The Jubilee Year

This in my opinion is one last opportunity to press the reset button to readjust for the rest of your life. According to the word of God, it is a significant season, one that many do not live to see, yet so loaded with great opportunities and blessings. A season that comes so quickly like a thief in the night and for many, our lives has carried us so far that we lose sight of the significance and blessings locked up in this season. The spiritual effect of this season is worth making the sacrifice to prepare for it, to expect it and pray for God to bring you into it. During my research of the jubilee year, I discovered five key blessings of the jubilee.

The Five Extraordinary Blessings of Jubilee

"And you shall hallow the fiftieth year, and proclaim liberty throughout all the land unto all the inhabitants thereof: it shall be a jubilee unto you; and you shall return every man unto his possession, and you shall return every man unto his family. *A jubilee shall that fiftieth year be unto you: you shall not sow, neither reap that which grows of itself in it, nor gather the grapes in it of your vine undressed. For it is the jubilee; it shall be holy unto you: you shall eat the increase thereof out of the field."* (Lev. 25:10–12 NKJV)

The People's Obligations

1. Holiness unto the LORD

   "And you shall hallow the fiftieth year and proclaim liberty throughout all the land unto all the inhabitants." (Lev. 25:10a and b NKJV)

   The year of Jubilee is the year of freedom and liberty unto all the inhabitants of the land. The seven obligations may be divided into two categories. Two of these are our obligations while five are the Lord's. First, we must strictly sanctify ourselves by living in righteousness and secondly, we must oppress no one. As a result, God liberates us from all forms of oppressions whether political or spiritual.

2. Freedom from Oppression

   "In the year of this jubilee you shall return every man unto his possession. And if you sell ought unto your neighbour, or buy ought of your neighbour's hand, you shall not oppress one another." (Lev. 25:13–14 NKJV)

   "You shall not therefore oppress one another; but you shall fear your God: for I am the LORD your God. Wherefore you shall do My statutes, and keep My judgments, and do them; and you shall dwell in the land in safety." (Lev. 25:17–19 NKJV)

   The second thing we must do is not to oppress one

another. In the year of Jubilee, it is forbidden to oppress anyone. We must love one another exceptionally this year. In the year of our Jubilee, we must love unconditionally our neighbours as ourselves including even our enemies. Love is the antidote against all forms of oppression. Why? The reason is that all the wickedness of man against man can be curtailed by love. All the commandments are fulfilled in love. All forms of oppression are due to lack of love.

"Owe no man anything, but to love one another: for he that loves another has fulfilled the law." (Rom. 13:8 NKJV)

"For this, You shall not commit adultery, You shall not kill, You shall not steal, You shall not bear false witness, You shall not covet; and if there be any other commandment, it is briefly comprehended in this saying, namely, You shall love your neighbour as yourself." (Rom. 13:9 NKJV)

This year of Jubilee we are liberated from all forms of fear and oppression whether emotional or spiritual. No one can oppress us by virtue of the proclamation of the Jubilee! Indeed, if we do not oppress anyone; no force, power or principality in heaven or earth can afflict us. I am amazed to see too many Christians captivated by the fear of many things.

As a result, you begin to fear and tremble because somebody puts a spell on you. Let me tell you, the simplest remedy for fear is love and faith in the living God. There is no greater power in heaven or on earth than the power that raised up Jesus Christ from the grave. If you are afraid of any demonic power, then your faith in God is small indeed. The power is not in the demons; it is in your fear because that which you fear will eventually come to pass in your life. (Job 3:25) It is the law. The law of faith works the same way; that which you believe with all your heart shall surely come to pass in your life.

"*Therefore, I say unto you, what things so ever you desire, when you pray, believe that you receive them, and you shall have them.*" (Mark 11:24 NKJV)

Now that we have covered the two obligations that we must do, let us examine the five extraordinary blessings that God will do for us in this year of Jubilee. Remember God promises to command these uncommon blessings upon us and upon the land if we will simply obey His commandments regarding the year of Jubilee.

The Father's Five Blessings

1. The "Proclamation of Liberty" upon all means that we are liberated from all bondages whether spiritual, financial, or even political captivity. (Lev. 25:10b; Luke 4:18 NKJV)
   "*And you shall hallow the fiftieth year, and proclaim liberty throughout all the land unto all the inhabitants thereof*" (Lev. 25:10b NKJV)
   "*… He has sent Me to bind up the broken hearted, to proclaim liberty to the captives, and the opening of the prison to them that are bound.*" (Isaiah 61:1b NKJV)
   Jesus Christ started His ministry by proclaiming the blessings

of the Jubilee upon His generation in His hometown synagogue in Bethlehem. He quoted directly from the book of Isaiah in Isaiah 61:1–2, almost verbatim.

"The Spirit of the Lord is upon Me, because He has anointed Me to preach the gospel to the poor; he hath sent me to heal the broken hearted, to preach deliverance to the captives, and recovering of sight to the blind, to set at liberty them that are bruised... to proclaim the acceptable year of the Lord." (Luke 4:18 NKJV)

Therefore, this year of JUBILEE, we can more assuredly proclaim our total LIBERTY! There is something unique about the JUBILEE; you must proclaim it in order to receive the blessing. God could have told us to pray about liberty, but He said, *"Proclaim liberty throughout all the land unto all the inhabitants thereof."* (Lev. 25:10b NKJV) Therefore, you must proclaim every one of these blessings of the JUBILEE upon yourself, your family and your nation, then allow God to command the blessings. These blessings are unique and unprecedented because they only happen maybe once or twice in the life of a man or woman of God. So, say to yourself out loud every morning: "This is my year of JUBILEE, therefore this is my year of total liberty in all ramifications of life in the name of Jesus Christ, Amen!"

2. *Every man shall return unto his possession; this speaks of RESTORATION.* (Lev. 25:10c NKJV)
   This year of Jubilee, everyone must possess his possession

as mandated by God through our Lord and Saviour, who is our JUBILEE! Everything must return to the original or rightful owner. No more are you a slave in your own land or heritage! The years of servitude and disenfranchisement are over. This is the year of JUBILEE therefore this is my year of total restoration.

3. *Every man shall return unto his family; this second mandate to return in this verse speaks of family RECONCILIATION.* (Lev. 25:10d NKJV)

   Many relationships have been severed as a result of severe hardships and injustice. This year of Jubilee promises total reconciliation between husband and wife, parents and children and even extended family relationships. Yes, this extends to the church of God and the household of faith as well. We expect an unprecedented level of cooperation between different pastors and various leaders in the larger body of Mashiach this year.

4. A year of Total REST from one's own works and rest from self-aggrandisements. (Lev. 25:11 and Mat. 11:28–30 NKJV) Jesus said, *"Come unto Me all ye that labour and are heavy laden and I will give you rest."*

   This mandate of the JUBILEE is unique and dynamic because it focuses on the poor who are often overworked and under-paid. Have you ever felt like you are always working and yet never quite able to make ends meet? Well then, proclaim JUBILEE upon yourself and Yahshua promises to set you free—He who the Son sets free is free indeed. Hallelujah! Cease from your own labour and take His yoke upon you and He will give you rest!

5. Unprecedented Divine Increase and Favour upon the land and the people. (Lev. 25:12 and 21 NKJV)
    Then I will command My blessing upon you in the sixth year, and it shall bring forth fruit for three years. WOW! God said that He will command His three-fold blessings of the JUBILEE upon us when we hallow the year of JUBILEE.
    You must proclaim these blessings of JUBILEE over yourself by faith. In other words, it does not matter what your past may have been; the failures, the disappointments and sheer hopelessness of the past do not count with God in the year of JUBILEE. God really is not moved by your past, but He regards your present act of faith or fear to determine your future. This is your year of jubilee, the acceptable year of the LORD. Proclaim it to yourself and say every waking morning as you look in the mirror: "This is my year of Jubilee; therefore, this is my year of unprecedented divine increase in Yahshua's name, Amen."

God is charting a totally new course of direction, a new paradigm shift for your life begins today.

Yes, this is your year of jubilee my friend, for the decree of the jubilee is already gone forth and its fulfilment is in Jesus.

"The Spirit of the Lord is upon Me, because He has anointed Me to preach the gospel to the poor; He has sent Me to heal the broken hearted, to preach deliverance to the captives, and recovering of sight to the blind, to set at liberty them that are bruised, to preach the acceptable year of the Lord." (Luke 4:18-19 NKJV)

"... This day is this scripture fulfilled in your ears." (Luke 4:21 NKJV)

The significance of the Jubilee year is not limited to just the rest of the land and rejuvenation of the soil. It is also to remind us, that the eternal Father is the Creator of the universe. And just as it took faith for the Israelites not to farm on the Jubilee years, so today it takes faith to trust Him for our sustenance in this year of our JUBILEE! Man is not the sole owner of the soil, neither is man the owner of the land solely but under the Almighty's trust.

"The land shall not be sold for ever: for the land is Mine; for you are strangers and sojourners with Me." (Lev. 25:23 NKJV)

Out of gratitude to the Father for our liberation, we must extend liberty to all our debtors and servants and release them in the year of JUBILEE.

"At the end of every seven years you shall make a release." (Deut. 15:1 NKJV)

The word translated "release" in Deuteronomy 15:1 can also mean "dropping". The seventh year is a year of dropping, or cancellation, of all debts. What better time than the JUBILEE year to settle old scores with people, to "bury the hatchet"?

Think for a moment of the extreme measure Yahshua went through to purchase us back from death to life. We were on a spiritual death row, waiting for execution in the lake of fire. Then, the Almighty in His great mercy through His only begotten Son, called us and forgave us. *"Through the Messiah, all charges were dropped against us for He blotted out the handwriting of ordinances that were against us and took them out of the way, nailing them to His cross."* (Col. 2:14 NKJV).

This alone should be a cause for jubilation and celebration.

When I discovered the above, I realised I had work to do in really preparing for my jubilee year and season. I was determined to align myself to receive these blessings that God has prepared for me. Even though I'm thankful for how far he has brought me, I realised there is far more to reach for and so I gird up my loins and this is the very reason you have this book in your hands so that you too can do the same. No matter your age right now, I need you to stop and assess your life, if you are below 50, you have such a great opportunity to use the pages of this book to guide you into your preparation so that you can enjoy your jubilee season.

"It's not the law of religion nor the principles of morality that define our highways and pathways to God; only by the Grace of God are we led and drawn to God. It is His grace that conquers a multitude of flaws and in that grace, there is only favour. Favour is not achieved; favour is received."

- C. Joy Bell C.

Chapter 1

Finding God

Jeremiah 29:11–14 (NKJV)

¹¹ For I know the thoughts that I think toward you, says the Lord, thoughts of peace and
not of evil, to give you a future and a hope.
¹² Then you will call upon Me and go and pray to Me, and I will listen to you.
¹³ And you will seek Me and find Me, when you search for Me with all your heart.
¹⁴ I will be found by you, says the Lord, and I will bring you back from your captivity; I will gather you from all the nations and from all the places where I have driven you, says the Lord, and I will bring you to the place from which I cause you to be carried away captive.

Your beginning point is finding God. Yes, finding God. There is a difference between going to church and knowing God. That knowing has a lot to do with our personal encounters with God, our experiences of Him. And please before you turn 50 you must find, know, encounter, and stick with God.

This may also sound so kindergarten, but I have lived long enough to tell you, you must find God and know God for real before you turn 50, because at 50 you need to be fully developing and deploying the very reason why God created you. Looking back in my life and thinking to myself when did it all change for better as I processed this journey called life? I realised it was when I found God on that faithful night of November 22, 1992.

I was invited to Green pastures Christian fellowship in the Finsbury park area by my cousin, prior to that time, I had always attended church with my parents back home but for me, I did not know God. I can categorically say I knew a religion but not a relationship with God—I simply did not know him.

By 50, you would have passed through different seasons of life, doing different things, chasing after different things, compromising because of different things, sinning because of different things, backslidden and re-converted, lukewarm and hot again, but by your jubilee year, there must be an assurance you have that if Christ came at any point, you will make it home safely.

Having a relationship with God can no longer be optional because you can never come into the fullness of anything without God. You will continue toiling and struggling and be engaged in the rat race of life without a rich relationship with your heavenly father.

2

The bible says in John 17: 3: "*And this is eternal life, that they know you the only true God, and Jesus Christ whom you have sent.*"

No matter how long you live, one day you will transition from this life, and you must decide as no one can do it for you where you want to transition to. I have come to realise that for me, knowing God has been a great source of strength as I have journeyed through life.

I have personally experienced *stability, acceptance, love, wisdom, healing, provision, protection, joy, peace, favour, access, fulfilment* and so much more from knowing God and these can never be traded for anything else.

I am still on that journey and I have not yet arrived but I can tell you that my life has become so much fuller, richer and makes more sense just because I know God. I can trace most of my accomplishments in life, my significance, those things that has brought me unexplainable pleasure and satisfaction to my relationship with God. I honestly do not know what my life would have been like at 50 if God was not a part of it. I gave my life to him in 1992 and this is 2020, you do the maths, and with all I have had to walk through, He has been there all the way.

I honestly believe I am God's favourite, when I look back, I could not attest it to anyone else but this amazing father who took a broken, rejected child and made her this amazing woman.

Finding God, loving God, knowing God and handing over your life to Him is solely your choice and your decision. No one can force you to love God, no one can push you to finding Him and sticking with him, you have to know you are in need of a saviour, you must want a different life other than that which you have, you must know that there is a bigger plan for your life from where it all began. No matter what your beginning was like; either good or bad, God has a better and richer plan for you and you must desire to know it and fulfil it.

I found God and even though that in itself was a process, I look back today and I could never have made it this far if He did not receive me, forgive me and has kept loving me since that fateful night when I surrendered to him.

Before we go on, let me ask you—and please don't
be quick to answer, do you know God? How?
Can you recall your salvation story?
What are your convictions of knowing God?

There are different reasons why people go in search of God. I believe there is something missing in us until we finally find Him, and it is after we have prayed the famous sinners prayer that the journey of finding and knowing God begins. Just because you pray a prayer does not mean you automatically know Him. Finding God is not a quick fix process nor is it a 100-metres dash. It is a lifetime relationship as he keeps unveiling different expressions of who He is as you seek Him more.

With regards to your jubilee season, it is very important that your relationship with God is sorted, that you are in communion with him on a consistent basis, that you have left your former lust behind, your former lifestyle, your sin conscious and active life—where it was all about how you felt and what you wanted.

There were some mistakes you might have made in your young wild days that you might have come to regret, the ignorance in which you walked, but as you come to this golden age, you need to begin to put your eternity in view. You must have a solid unwavering, compromise and sin-free relationship with your heavenly father.

Finding and knowing God:

Gives your life genuine meaning

Reveals you to you i.e. your identity

Reveals his masterplan for your life

Heals you from your past pain

Delivers you from your old destructive self

Makes a new way for you even if it looks as if there is no way out

Changes your perspective to live completely

Gives you the desires of your heart that is according to His will for you

Totally changes you forever

Gives you boldness and confidence to face any season or situation

Please let me be clear, we will fall short sometimes on this journey, so my message is not one of self-righteousness but one of a personal revelation and conviction of not just who God is, but that you are His child and He loves you and has a plan for your life.

It is about fully embracing your adoption by the blood of Jesus; it is about committing the totality of your life to Him and trusting that He will do what is best for you. It is about honouring Him, seeking Him with all your heart, worshiping Him, serving Him and advancing His purposes above yours. It is deeper than just going to a building called church without knowing Him. It is about loving Him, wanting Him, waiting on Him, hearing Him and obeying Him.

It involves surrendering every aspect of your life to Him, understanding His ways and how He wants you to be, think, act, and what He wants you to do in every situation. It is about making Him the Ruler and the Lord of your life.

At 50, you must have this in place. You cannot be stuck in your old self, your old ways, old desires, old pleasures of life or your old sinful ways. You must have reached a point in life where you know you are desperately in need of a saviour.

What are those things that you still question about God's redemption plan for your life?

In your jubilee year, you must first hallow the year of

Jubilee and live holy and righteous lives unto the LORD. (Lev. 25:10a; Luke 4:18a NKJV). This is a significant requirement of your jubilee years hence a key reason why you must find God before you turn 50. Many times we think to live holy is about restraining ourselves, or the apparel we wear, or the jewellery we do not wear, but really living Holy is simply living a life that is in agreement with God's word and preference and if that includes Him telling you to refrain from some things, then so be it.

But the main thing here is to ask if you agree and align with God. By the time you are celebrating your jubilee year, your thirst for worldliness and friendship with the world should have diminished if not totally eradicated, because as I will be sharing with you later, you must be consumed with the purpose of God for your life which in itself will place some restrictions on you.

You will find out that the deeper friendship you have with God, the less your love for the world and the things of the world. You cannot love God and love the world the Bible says. In the book of Matthew, it says you cannot serve two masters—you will love one and hate the other. So, by 50 there is a decision to make on who is going to have your affection and focus. Is it going to be God or the world?

"Whoever has my commandments and keeps them he it is who loves me. And he who loves me will be loved by my father and I will love him and manifest myself to him." (John 14:21 NKJV)

7

I want you to write some of your worldly struggles down. For those reading this book and are yet to be 50, please start the process of eradicating it, for those who are 50 and above reading this, you are left with no other choice but to eradicate it now so you can pursue the purpose of God for your life.

Getting to know God also requires you developing some disciplines with God, such as studying the word. Believe it or not, this has become a major issue for many Christians. Life seems to be so busy that reading our Bibles has become an overwhelming issue, this should not be so if we understand the critical importance of the word and how it should align our lives to the will, plan, desires and precepts of God. Reading our Bibles should become to us as breathing air to service our body because this is what services our lives.

"Men shall not live by bread alone but by every word that proceeds from the mouth of God." (Matthew 4:4 NKJV) If you lack understanding of the word of God how then do you understand your life or how God wants to govern it?

"Your word is a lamp unto my feet and a light unto my path." (Psalm 119:105 NKJV)

"Do your best to present yourself to God as one approved, a worker who has no need to be ashamed, rightly handling the word of truth." (2 Timothy 2:15 NKJV)

8

I see a lot of people in their 40s and 50s who still don't see the vital importance of the word and why they must have an intimate fellowship with the word. You only know God through his word and if you cannot make time for His word, how will you grow in Him, understand Him, be sensitive to his voice, know His ways and act accordingly?

Yes, knowing God is a lifetime journey, but please start on time. Don't live a life of confusion, oppression, frustration, stress without Christ and the knowledge of his word. Make it a lifestyle today—now this moment, stop excusing it, you will never be truly, successfully fulfilled without God. You don't have to do it on your own, you don't have to struggle your way through, a way has been made for you in Christ and the price has been paid. Don't play now and pay later, pay now so you can play well later, develop a daily love for his word, reading, meditating, and confessing.

What's your relationship with the word of God?
How much time in your life right now do you spend
with the word?
What's the hinderance you are facing?

Even though the first step is finding God, the next one will be staying connected to Him. Life has a way of making us lose sight of God sometimes, we get overly busy and forget that according to Galatians 2:20, we have been crucified with Christ and the life we now live, we live in him who loved us and died for us. I realised on my journey to jubilee that it takes intentionality and dedication from a place of deep love to remain consistent in God—where He is still a high priority in your life, where you will not give Him up for other things.

His greatest desire is for intimacy and relationship with us. He does not want us to continue using Him for our own selfishness; where we only pray when we need him, fast when we need him or study when we need him. That is not right. He wants a continuous, consistent, fervent loving relationship with us. This is so key because as I have said earlier and is worth saying again, everything else aligns from our knowledge through our relationship with our Father.

He loves to be sought after. He wants to be loved, adored, worshipped, exalted, consulted and inquired of. He wants to be our all in all, the alpha and the omega, the very centre of our being. Coming to 50, reality of life dawns on you in a very profound way and the Lord begins to require more of you and from you, to grow in your seeking, knowledge, and intimacy with God. As you desire to simplify your life at this golden age, you must also simplify the business that cuts you away from your relationship with God. You must begin to take time away with Him seriously. You must seek after His heart more, His desires more, His plans more, His ways more.

One of the biggest blessings of me finding God and keeping that loving consistent relationship is FORGIVENESS. I have had things hit me in life that I needed to forgive and be forgiven and my biggest joy from my relationship with God is the gift of forgiveness. Yes, gift as I have realised that forgiveness is a gift that you are given and that you have the honour to give to others.

Forgiveness is big for me because I am one who hates injustice and I fight every form of injustice but in my journey as a child of God, I learned from receiving His forgiveness to be able to forgive others who trespass against me. As I prepare for my jubilee year, I find this important to my being able to access many blessings in my jubilee season.

I want you to think about your own journey and examine where you are at right now with the Lord. Do you truly know him? Daniel 11:32 says, "They that know their God shall be strong and do great exploits." That word "know" connotes experiential knowledge derived by intimacy. Reflect on this for a while and write down your challenges at this level of your life.

*"Unless we base our
sense of identity upon
the truth of who we are,
it is impossible to attain
true happiness."*
- Dr Steve Maraboli

Chapter 2

Identity

THE QUESTION I'm about to ask might seem like an irrelevant question to ask at this point of your life, but I have worked with women long enough and know people on a personal level who at over 50 years of age, are struggling with who they really are.

Who are you really? Please do not give me any spiritual jargons but dig deep to ask yourself.

Another blessing I have received from knowing God is that I have discovered who I truly am, I have come to love and accept the person God has created me to be. I know without a shadow of doubt that God loves me, that I have been fearfully and wonderfully made, that he has carefully woven me uniquely with all my gifts, abilities, potentials, personality and character for a specific purpose for His kingdom agenda.

Many have lived for decades on a faulty identity, one that has been plagued with disappointments, failure, failed expectations, abuse etc. We were a perfect plan altered by life, but I believe when you become a believer in Christ, you must first invest in your journey and process of discovering your true identity that was lost when man fell. Who you believe you are and how you see yourself will determine what you will do with your life.

Understanding and embracing your identity is important in every aspect of your life. You cannot function well if you have a wrong picture of yourself. How you see yourself determines what you do with and for you. As a mentor, I am still shocked at the answers people give when they are asked, who are you? Or who do you believe you really are? Many come up with a one-liner, some with a lot of responses that proves that they have not thought deep enough about their true identity but are just trying to fit in someone else's perception but not their own true believe.

We fall into the wrong friendships, marriages, ventures etc because we lack the understanding of who we have been created to be and the unique gifts and potentials we are loaded with.

There is a clear picture God has given us in his word to live up to as our proper and right identity. It is found in the book of 1 Peter 2:9 and we quote this scripture so often but the question here is, have you stopped, to really think about it? Is it your honest reality or are you still playing lip service with it? How much of your life emulates this scripture?

Our background has played a huge part in how we have ended up with our present identity, it could be you were born into a family where you were never...,

Acknowledged

Celebrated

Loved

Affirmed

Supported

And you have grown up not thinking much of yourself or your uniqueness, but I keep saying it, when you come into Christ the rule of the game must change. You must intentionally first begin the journey of wholesomeness to get back your true self so you can know what your life is about and how you must become all God had pre-ordained for you.

For some of you that will be able to relate with this book, you have probably left your salvation till this late but by the jubilee age of 50, you must know who you truly are. You must know who God has made you to be and not still living in the faulty identity of our parents. You must know the uniqueness in which God has made you, you must have gone through some thorough dimension of inner healing and freedom to get rid of the pain that brought about the dysfunctional identity and the new person who is rich in the love of Christ.

"One of the greatest tragedies in life is to lose your authentic self and accept the version of you that is expected by everyone else." – K.L Toth

Here are some basic reasons why people lose their identity:
1. Putting other people's needs before theirs. This behaviour can lead to self-neglect and diminished self-worth.

2. Detachment from your thoughts and feelings. A myriad of distractions exists that may be used to disconnect us from "the world": alcohol, drugs, food and even electronics.

3. Experiencing a life-changing event or transition. Trauma is one example—the death of a loved one, job loss, divorce— these and other circumstances can derail us from our true selves.

4. Repressing and subsequently "burying" our real selves out of shame, embarrassment or fear. Sometimes, because we have been subjected to bullying and criticism, we make conscious or unconscious decisions to hide our true selves after such treatment.

When we lose our identity and sense of self, we are likely to seek our sense of self-worth from others. It suddenly becomes very important how others view us, as our sense of value, self-worth and our feelings of confidence, are dependent on external factors such as our physical appearance, success, status, money, and even fame. As a result, we seek reassurance and praise from others to feel okay about ourselves but, our emotional well-being depends on how we feel about ourselves.

Our sense of self—our "identity"—should not come from what others think about us. We shouldn't allow people's comment on how we look, or how we behave affect us but because we worry about being judged or measured by others (and falling short of their requirements), we put on an act, a facade, a mask. We all do it at times, present the "best-self" out there, when inside, we may be feeling very different to the real "us" hiding underneath. However, when this happens all the time, it could be a problem.

Such dependency on external validation prevents the real "you" from being out there, it affects your personal growth, as well as the opportunity for happiness. Low self-esteem can be linked to issues from the past, from childhood and parental neglect, from abuse and trauma, from childhood bullying, and this often shapes how we view ourselves and how we interact with others.

I was a child born into a polygamous family with very little love from my father. I was never affirmed, acknowledged, supported, guided, or given any start in life from a male perspective or a fatherly perspective. As a matter of fact, I am not sure I knew who I was until when I was in my 30s. Many children's identities get ruined even before they know what life is about. I had no understanding of fatherhood who is meant to be the one that establishes the identity of the family, the order of the family, I did not have that. My mother did a great job compensating for my father's absence but as I grew, I realised that the presence of a father is a major part of a child's foundation and that was missing in my own case. It will take only the grace and the mercy of God coupled with your own intentionality to be healed and be revealed all over again.

Your journey as a believer is that of redemption and restoration back to God's original plan and design to accomplish his divine purpose. You cannot run away from your true self; you have an obligation to discover it and fulfil it.

17

This issue of identity crisis is the foundational problem in our world today and it is being transitioned from one generation to the other. We now have a generation of young people with no hope in life; they are battered, angry, confused, non-achievers—all stemming from the truth of a lack of knowledge. That is why finding God is so key, you cannot find yourself until you first find Him. He is the revealer of your true identity. Knowing God is your beginning point of correcting some messed up notion about yourself, that is where you get answers to your confusion and a reassurance of the new person He wants to make you into. 2 Corinthians 5:17 says when you come into Christ you are a new creation, old things are passed away, all things have become new, the old nature has been stripped off and you now have the opportunity to clothe yourself in the new nature of God.

Our struggles started because the adults that were meant to have raised us as children in the way of the Lord so that when we grow we will not depart from it, were themselves lost in the sea of identity crisis. This has become the catalyst for dysfunctional homes and families which in turn is resulting into dysfunctional communities and nations. Change will only come when each of us pay the price to discover our real selves and develop and deploy that true person locked up on the inside so that we can begin to make positive contributions to help the next generation.

Our identity gives us relevance,

Understanding

Positioning

Access

Authority

Influence

Experience

Capacity

Favour

Impact

And so much more. It is the strength of our engagement with the kingdom of God and please by 50, you must have walked a journey of embracing with full understanding, who God calls and sees you as.

What is your own story of where the dysfunctional identity started?

You must put whatever might have caused dysfunctional identity in your life behind you as you plan to come into your season of jubilee. You must intentionally make sure you deal with any issues that can alter your identity. We should realise that no matter what life throws at us, it must never leave us doubting the sovereignty of God or his thoughts and plans of who he has made us to be and how he has packaged us.

It is never too early to start this process of restoring your real self, whether you are in your 20s or 40s. Please start now!

19

Have a solid place in yourself that remains constant regardless of what may happen in your journey in life. Do you know that no matter what you face in life it does not remove the root of the family you came out from? Your maiden name remains forever, whether you are married or not, whether you experienced trauma, pain or any negative circumstances in life or not, your maiden name is a permanent constant in your life. Your identity in Christ not in your own self, must remain constant in your life as well.

That is why I love the scriptures in Romans 12:1–3, you will have to read it yourself. When you know who you are, you will watch what and who you conform to. You will realise how special and unique you are and so, you will not participate in some things that the world is participating in, you will not degrade yourself, but will carry yourself with dignity and poise. You will also be able to know the good, acceptable and perfect will of God.

How well do you know yourself?

You must believe and act upon the truth of who you already know God has created you to be. You must learn to walk through life from a constant place of knowing who you are and whose you are.

Having a true understanding of your God identity and

embracing it helps you to begin to identify your unique qualities, gifts, abilities, special qualities and these are all important in your ability to live a wholesome and fulfilled life.

Jealousy, envy and low self-esteem are all products of identity crises that the enemy has jumped on to keep us in a place of perpetual pain and discomfort. Jesus wants us free from these encumbrances so we can run the race of life that is set before us and win. We have a big question to ask ourselves in life that if we are totally dependent on our understanding of who we are and whose we are, what then do we want out of life? This cannot be taken lightly because I have lived long enough to meet people who either don't have a clue, or they have a very disjointed view of life in general that robs them of the ability to see a preferred future. We all want different things in life, yes, I agree but please make sure you have a holistic view and that you are seeing life through God's lenses and perspective, so that you don't self-sabotage.

You cannot see yourself as a failure, useless, good for nothing person, have a "can't achieve anything" mindset and have a healthy desire for life. You must first see yourself as God sees you in 1 Peter 2:9 and embrace that royal status before you can clearly look at your life in totality and have some great things you want your life to stand for. You are a meaningful specific not a wandering generality. Wake up to your real self, 50 is your last opportunity to reset for the rest of your life and you cannot reset on a faulty foundation.

—————————— ✿ ——————————

Have you been able to answer the question: "What do you want out of life?"

Can you take a minute now and identify some of your unique traits?

What does your inner critic tell you about these traits?

Now, can you make an attempt to describe who you believe you should be?

———————————————————————————————————

I want you to understand and grasp that you will never be like everybody else. If God created us all to be the same, life will be incredibly boring. You are a meaningful specific, you can't continue living a life where you are too busy trying to be someone else that you forget who you are and how special He has made you. I struggled for years to fit into different people's boxes and I can tell you it's overwhelming and a waste of life and time. But when I started to really deal with the issues of the heart and those things that bruised my heart so much that I lost touch with my true self, a new level of love and boldness came over me.

I listed down all the traits I identified, even the one I thought through other people's opinion were negative, I found out in God's hands they became my greatest strength. One of them is my ability to talk and communicate; others call it being talkative, loud, boisterous etc., but to my God, He gave me a unique ability to relate to people, to talk, to teach, to train and equip people to discover and develop their God given abilities so they can be a better witness for Him. Imagine if I left myself internally damaged, compounded by people's opinion which has no relevance with how or what God has made me to be, many that I have been called to witness to will miss out on this gift I have been given.

Until you take that intentional journey of finding you, your life will be about living other people's false and unfounded ideology of who they think you should be.

Take a moment and write your example of what you have believed about yourself that is only founded on other people's opinion. How has these shaped your life?

What cultural labels have you accepted about your identity?

Now by the time you turn 50, what do you need to change to come into your God given identity?

Who will you like to see emerge?

What are you willing to do at all costs to emerge with this new identity?

These are few scriptures to meditate on to remind you of who God says you are:

Genesis 1:27

"So, God created man in his own image, in the image of God he created him; male and female he created them."

2 Corinthians 5:17

"Therefore, if anyone is in Christ, he is a new creation. The old has passed away; behold, the new has come."

1 Peter 2:9

"But you are a chosen race, a royal priesthood, a holy nation, a people for his own possession, that you may proclaim the excellencies of him who called you out of darkness into his marvellous light."

Jeremiah 1:5

"Before I formed you in the womb I knew you, and before you were born I consecrated you; I appointed you a prophet to the nations."

Jeremiah 29:11

"For I know the plans I have for you, declares the LORD, plans for welfare and not for evil, to give you a future and a hope."

Galatians 2:20

"I have been crucified with Christ. It is no longer I who live, but Christ who lives in me. And the life I now live in the flesh I live by faith in the Son of God, who loved me and gave himself."

Values

As you walk the journey of the restoration of your true identity, you must take a stop at the road of your values This forms a huge part of your renewed identity. You have to analyse those value systems you have operated in all your life, how you came to accepting those values, who gave them to you, how have they affected your life and now that you are in Christ Jesus, are you still operating those old ideologies and values?

What are values? Values are deep-seated **beliefs** about what is right or wrong and about what is important or unimportant. They are principles, standards or qualities that people care about and that contribute to driving people's behaviours.

Beliefs are the convictions that we generally hold to be true, usually without actual proof or evidence.

Beliefs are basically assumptions that we make about the world and our values stem from those beliefs. Our values are things that we deem important and they can include concepts like: equality, honesty, education, effort, perseverance, loyalty, faithfulness, conservation of the environment and many other concepts.

Our beliefs grow from what we see, hear, experience, read and think about. From these things, we develop an opinion that we hold to be true and unmovable at that time. From our beliefs we derive our values, which can either be correct or incorrect when compared with evidence, but nonetheless hold true for us.

It is possible for our beliefs and values to differ over time as we encounter evidence or have experiences that challenge our previously held views. Conversely our beliefs and values can also be strengthened by experience or evidence. For example, someone who believes in God might have that belief confirmed when they see a loved one recover from cancer and see it as a miracle from God. However, a person might have their belief in the essential goodness of human beings shaken and changed if they have a truly terrible experience.

Everyone has an internalised system of beliefs and values that they have developed throughout their lives, it becomes a standard for understanding the world around them, directing and justifying their own actions, sustaining their attitudes and, inevitably, judging others' actions. Values can be abstract, such as freedom of choice, or specific, relating to, for example, hunger, poverty or racism.

Personal Values

You will now explore personal values and how these have an impact on your interests and choices you make in life.

Personal values stem from our social background, religion (if we have one), ethnic origin, culture, upbringing, education and our experiences of life and work. Personal values are not static. They continue to evolve during our lifetime as we experience new situations and people's behaviours, particularly ones involving conflict or difference, or ones we find surprising or offensive.

These encounters provide opportunities to question and rethink our own values. Of course, people may not be fully conscious of the values they hold or of the value judgments they are making when taking particular actions. People are also not necessarily consistent in their behaviour, and there may be a discrepancy between what we say our values are and how we act.

1. What is important to you?
2. What are the values that run your life as at now?
3. What are the beliefs you have held on to for now?

   Have they helped you, can they continue to help you move forward? What must change?
4. What circumstances of life can you remember that has rocked or shaped your values or beliefs? Can you identify any lessons learnt?

As I approach my season of jubilee, I am identifying values and beliefs that are no longer relevant to this season of my life, because as I mentioned earlier, our values and beliefs evolve as we get older and our circumstances in life changes us—all of a sudden we realise that what got us here may not take us there.

What got you to this point may no longer be relevant or enough to take you further in life, so as everything else that changes or is subject to change, you must carefully look at your behaviours, attitudes, values and beliefs and make the necessary changes now to prepare you for your next season. I keep saying it but if you are younger than 50 and you are reading this workbook, my biggest message for you is for you to plan and change NOW. Don't overlook any area of your preparation and your change.

Behaviours (How you act): Usually reflects your values, beliefs and attitudes but can be influenced by other factors e.g. the attitudes and behaviours of others, convenience, economics, environment etc.

Attitudes (How you express your values and beliefs through words and actions: This is made up of three components namely: Cognitive – what we believe; Affective – our feelings; Behaviour – learned associations.

Values (What you value, or think is important): Principles in our lives that guide our decision making e.g. honesty, loyalty, equality etc.

Beliefs (Ideas that you hold to be true, even if unproven or irrational): Developed from what we see, hear, experience, read and think about.

5. I need you to identify both the positive and negative behaviours and attitudes that has stemmed from your beliefs and values. Assess its impact on your life and relationships.

Core Values About Life

Often, when you hear someone discuss why they fell in love with their other half, they will mention that they have the same values. In this case, they are often talking about core values, or internal beliefs that dictate how life should be lived.

Core beliefs are the fundamental convictions we have about ourselves; they are the absolute truths we have adopted throughout the course of our entire lives, usually starting in childhood.

Some examples of core values people might have about life include the following:

- A belief, or lack thereof, in God or an affiliation with a religious/spiritual institution
- A belief in being a good steward of resources and in exercising frugality
- A belief that family is of fundamental importance
- A belief that honesty is always the best policy and that trust has to be earned
- A belief in maintaining a healthy work/life balance

To get a sense of what your core values are, ask yourself what activities bring you the most joy, or what you could not live without. What gives your life meaning or what do you want to achieve? If you can articulate those answers, you'll likely see a pattern that you can boil down into a single concept, such as a consistently positive attitude or using your creativity to make the world a better place.

6. What are the main core beliefs you can identify that has affected your life negatively?

7. How have you responded in life to this core beliefs i.e. what character attribute can you identify with it?

8. What is the new belief you are going to adopt to mitigate the core belief?

9. From all we have been discussing can you identify what your personal convictions in life from now will be? This is because conviction is the next step of belief that proves there is no turning back.

10. What are some of the core values for you in this season? Explain what role they will play in your life for the new season and why. Feel free to choose from the list below or add yours if they are not included.

Here are some examples of core values from which you may wish to choose:

• Dependability
• Reliability

- Loyalty
- Commitment
- Open-mindedness
- Consistency
- Honesty
- Efficiency
- Innovation
- Creativity
- Good humour
- Compassion
- Spirit of adventure
- Motivation
- Positivity
- Optimism
- Passion
- Respect
- Fitness
- Courage
- Education
- Perseverance
- Patriotism
- Service to others
- Environmentalism

My core values have changed a bit as I approach this new season. I used to be very keen on friendship. I was one who did not know how to separate acquaintances from real friends.

I treated everyone the same way and expected the same from them but I was seriously disappointed and betrayed to the point that I wrote a book about my experiences with friendship. The book is titled, *Before I Call You My Friend*. Get yourself a copy, it will bless you. So now that I am turning 50, even though my core belief in friendship still stands, I have tweaked my behaviours, attitudes and values with regards to those who I will call my friends.

11. **Can you identify an area in your life that your value may still be relevant but your other elements i.e. behaviour etc. needs to change? Write about it and include what exactly needs to change because this exercise will support you to make the necessary changes.**

So, you have answered all these questions and you are beginning to wonder where to start. You are saying to yourself: "How do I make this transition? I can see that I am living way below God's ordained standard, ability and potential." Now, this is where investment in your life must begin for personal growth and development. Culturally, as an African, I have realised that a great number of us do not invest in ourselves, and for some, it is only if money is at the end of the game.

However, part of living a flourishing and fulfilling life is in your ability to invest in yourself.

Investment is required for every area of your life and you must settle that, but I also want you to focus on your personal growth and development.

Investing in Yourself

There is no age limit to when you can start investing in yourself. For example, if you have a secondary school or university degree, you have invested somewhat in yourself. However, I have also discovered that the key principle of living your best life is not part of the school curriculum, you will have to go in search of a good mentor who is living the results of this life principles to take you on this journey of self-discovery and development. If you are still younger than 50, I want to encourage you to start NOW. Yes, now! It is a journey and the earlier you start, the better you will be by the time you turn 50.

Investing in your personal growth and development is important, nothing just happens by chance. As someone once said, "if you fail to plan, then you have planned to fail."

When you know who you are, you are more inclined to make that person you have discovered a better person in every way. That is why I am a passionate supporter of personal development; you must develop yourself because this helps you identify what is called the swot analysis.

Strengths

Weaknesses

Opportunities

Threats

Personal development covers activities that improve awareness and identity, **develop** talents and potential, build human capital and facilitate employability, enhance the quality of life and contribute to the realisation of dreams and aspirations.

It takes you on a journey of discovery, deliverance, development and deployment. It makes you aware, it opens you up to new opportunities, it increases your knowledge and confidence, it helps your understanding and discernment, it shapes your character and it corrects your perspective. The opportunity of personal development is vast and as a mentor, leaving this aspect of your life till later rather than sooner has negative results. One is the fact that you would have lost a lot of grounds, opportunities, networks, relationships, information, and knowledge that could probably have made your journey a richer and more fruitful one.

It is a sad thing that I have noticed, many do not see the value or seize the opportunity of self-development. It is more than just money; it is giving yourself a well-rounded holistic life that is flourishing and fruitful.

Personal development shows you where you are and where you need to get to and how you need to get there.

There are 6 core benefits of personal development, they are:

- Self-awareness – what do you want out of your life?

- A sense of direction – once you know what you want, clarify how you will get it.
- Improved focus and effectiveness
- More motivation
- Greater resilience
- More fulfilling relationships

Personal development provokes questions that are deep and shines a light on the essence of living and awakens your full potential as human beings.

If you would like to maximise the benefits of self-reflection, ask yourself questions that provoke your mind and force you to reconsider the way you live and the way you look at the world. The best questions to ask ourselves are those that would usher in a new perspective and remind us of who we are, as well as who we aspire to be. They are questions that tend to become inner voices of wisdom, guiding us through the turbulent journey of life.

Here are a few of those questions to ask yourself:
1. **Are you living the life you desire and dreamt about? If not, why?**
2. **What scares you the most about your future?**
3. **When last did you push the boundaries of your comfort zone?**

Self-Improvement

An important element of personal growth and development is self-improvement. You must be improving from year to year. It is not a compliment when people see you and tell you, you have not changed. You must strive daily to change certain areas and aspects of your life, that is the proof of your growth. Self-improvement is the improvement of one's knowledge, status, or character by one's own efforts.

Stagnation stinks, so you do not want your life to stagnate. Many are in that place of stagnation and so there is no desire, desperation or realisation that some things must change. Unfortunately, their environment does not wake them from that slumber of stagnation neither do the people who are close to them. Everyone seems to be stuck doing the same old yet expecting a different result.

"The greatest of all miracles, is that we need not be tomorrow what we are today." This is why self-improvement is key for your jubilee season, to daily invest in and sacrifice in improving yourself. You need to recognise that we have a potential to keep improving and making progress until the day we die. What got you here is not capable of taking you there. What got you to 50 cannot take you to 60, there must be definite intentional adjustments you should factor into your life to encourage a daily change in you.

Here are few ways to improve consistently and I need you to embed these truths into your life daily. Stop doing the same old things you have always done; improvement begins when you start to do those things you could and should do.

Now take a moment and write down some things you can and should begin to do from now on.

Stop doing only what is expected of you, you will plateau, start doing more than what is expected of you in every area of your life. We live in a world that celebrates attendance more than contributions and this informs the mind with a lie, to make one feel you are doing well just because you are doing what is expected. By your jubilee, your life should be ready for this new season of new adventure and impact and this is available by going the extra mile. Doing more develops a habit of excellence in your life.

Now write down a few things you would do more of, as you prepare for this new season.

Develop a lifestyle of doing important things relating to your destination daily and not occasionally. To advance towards your destination, you must constantly do things that are geared towards your progress. These things must be the right and important things.

If you knew you could not fail, what would you attempt?

If you had no limitations of any sort, what would you like to do?

If you had all the money you need, what would you be doing with your life?

Reflection – Take this time to reflect on this chapter and write out your thoughts and instructions from the Lord.

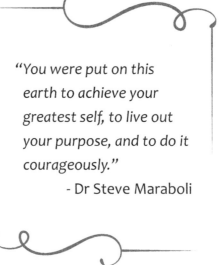

"You were put on this earth to achieve your greatest self, to live out your purpose, and to do it courageously."

- Dr Steve Maraboli

Chapter 3

Purpose

"You made all the delicate, inner parts of my body and knit me together in my mother's womb. Thank you for making me so wonderfully complex. Your workmanship is marvellous— how well I know it. You watched me as I was being formed in utter seclusion, as I was woven together in the dark of the womb. You saw me before I was born. Every day of my life was recorded in your book. Every moment was laid out before a single day had passed." (Psalms 139:13–16 NKJV)

"The purpose of life is not to be happy. It is to be useful, to be honourable, to be compassionate, to have it make some difference that you have lived and lived well."
— Ralph Waldo Emerson

Your personal development leads you into the fulfilment of your purpose. When you invest in personally developing

39

yourself, you receive tools and tips to help you begin to take the necessary steps towards understanding and fulfilling your purpose.

You have been created on purpose for a purpose, you were not created because God was bored. You were not just created because your parents wanted children, you were specifically planned and crafted by God because he had a preordained plan for your life. Jeremiah 1:5 talks about this. Many people are struggling through life trying to survive in life, trying to live out their so-called dreams, piercing themselves with too many sorrows because they have not come into the knowledge of why God created them. I realise life can pass you by without a purpose that for some, it becomes too late to realise that they have not done anything towards their eternal glory before death comes for them. We are all living life but my biggest message in this book is for you to find out from God why you are here.

This is one of the key questions we try to answer in our discovery class, why am I here? To do what? For what? There is more to us than marriage, having children, buying homes, going on vacations, partying around, going to a building every Sunday we call church, building friendships etc. There is a bigger plan in the heart of the father. In Genesis 1:26–28 we were all given a mandate to multiply, have dominion, subdue, be in charge till the Lord comes back. You have a huge responsibility in seeking the father to find out what you are meant to multiply, subdue, have dominion over until He returns.

We have been made the light of the world and the salt of the earth, so the question is where and how? Your greatest discovery in life will be to discover your God ordained purpose and your greatest achievement will be to fulfil it. When you look through the entire bible, you will find out that it is loaded with stories of ordinary lives that became purposeful lives— that is the order of God.

How is purpose defined? It is defined as the reason why we do something or why something exists. We exist here on earth to carry out our father's mandate. God has a mandate and it is His children that should be executing His mandate. Your personality, gifts, natural talents, passion have all been carefully packaged in you for your purpose in life. You cannot live your own life the way you want and expect His eternity. The best of my life till my mid 30s was about what I want and how I wanted it. There were so many desires that never was realised until we were introduced to late Dr Myles Monroe and his ministry in the early 2000s and he began to mentor my husband and I. We would travel yearly to the Bahamas to sit at his feet and learn the message of the kingdom of God and His purpose.

That was our eye-opening years of coming to the realisation that God truly has a plan for our lives. Although two months into our (my husband and I) wedding in July 1995, a great prophet of God by the name of Dick Mills came to our church then and prophesied what has become our purpose today as a couple to us.

You will keep seeing your life as a hit and miss until you discover your purpose. You can never find fulfilment until you discover purpose. There is great joy in fulfilling your purpose, there is great reward and self-accomplishment in a purpose-driven life. Our lives should not be aimless if we call ourselves God's children. Our lives should daily enrich and empower others through the discovery of the grace and call of God upon us to live a life that is impacting and advancing His agenda. Without a vision, my people cast off restraint— yes, without a purpose, there is no priority, no focus, no right development, no positioning, and no blessing. That is a wasted life in my view. One of my greatest pain is seeing many people in their 50s still stuck in the rat race of life, with no direction as to how they can be developed to make an impact in their generation, how they can live a life of quality and fulfilment, touching others. Many are consumed with the day to day needs of life—what shall I eat, drink, and put on? It is sadder when we claim to be Christians yet invest nothing in understanding and discovering our God-given purpose. Your purpose is everything. It is the very reason why you are here, and you must get this now, so you don't keep wasting valuable time.

You might want to ask, "how do I know my purpose?" My answer for you is in Jeremiah 29:11–14. God is the master planner for your life and if you seek Him with all your heart, He will reveal what your life purpose is. You already have the basics in you, He just needs to point you to it. I have seen many in their 50s still running the rat race of life diligently and yet to discover their God-given race. The rat race of life has no eternal value and you will only receive your crown if you finish your assignment. Which is why at 50, I'm thankful that I have come into a good knowledge of why God created me.

The passion, personality, mindset, gifts and talents, capacity and all he has packaged me with has been a great sustenance to my call to facilitate transformation first to women, then men in helping to support or activate their deliverance, discovery, development and deployment of their God-given potentials so that they can be better witnesses for God in their homes, communities and ultimately in the nations of the world.

We are all born with a deep and meaningful purpose that we must discover. Your purpose is not something you need to make up; it is already there. You have to uncover it in order to **create the life you want**. You may ask yourself, "what is my purpose in life?" You can begin to discover your passion or your purpose by exploring some things.

My journey of purpose started in the year 2000 when I founded a women's group called the Lydia group, it was the first time I heard God clearly give me instructions concerning my purpose which is to facilitate training and transformation for women so they can discover, develop and deploy their God potential to be a better witness in their homes, communities and nations of the world. It was like hands fitting a glove, I realised that something I had loved to do as a child was gathering girls to play and the passion with which I was always looking for solutions for others, prompting them to do things

43

differently etc. was really my purpose in God. I have to say, purpose is a journey and as you discover yourself more, you begin to discover what God has for you and how you will fulfil the mandate for your life. Please let me say again here that you must discover this purpose, many are going through life without a knowledge of what God has planned for them and truth be told, even those who are over the age of 50 still have no clue about who they are or what they are meant to do.

Let this be an awakening for you to make sure you know who you are and what you are here to do.

1. Before we start the exploring, I do not want to generalise, so I ask you, do you know your purpose? Do you have any understanding whatsoever of what your purpose in life is?
2. What do you love to do? Be very descriptive.
3. What comes easily to you that you are not satisfied with and you wish you can change?
4. What are the two qualities that you most enjoy?
5. What are the ways you enjoy expressing these qualities the most?
6. What have you contributed to your community up till now? Give details of any humanitarian or community project you have significantly contributed to.

Benefits of a Purpose Driven Life:

- Knowing your purpose gives meaning to your life—without God, life has no purpose; without purpose, life has no meaning; without meaning, life has no significance or hope; and hope comes from knowing and fulfilling your purpose in life.

- Knowing your purpose simplifies your life—it defines what you do and what you do not do. Your purpose becomes the standard with which you evaluate which activities are essential and which are not. Without a clear purpose, you have no foundation on which you base your decisions, which leads you to making choices based on circumstances, pressures, and your momentary mood.

- Knowing your purpose helps you to focus—it concentrates your effort and energy on what is important. You become effective at being selective. Without a purpose, you will keep changing directions, jobs, relations, churches, or other external factors hoping each change will settle the confusion or fill the emptiness in your heart.

- Knowing your purpose motivates you—purpose always produces passion.
  On the other hand, passion dissipates when you lack purpose. Nothing energises you like a clear purpose.

- Knowing your purpose prepares you for eternity—many people spend their lives trying to create a legacy on the earth. They want to be remembered when they are gone. Yet what ultimately matters is not what others says about you but what God says. A wiser use of time is to build an eternal legacy. We all must stand one day and give account of our lives.

7. What are you passionate about?
8. Have you done anything tangible with that passion? E.g. feed the orphans, support widows, serve the underprivileged etc.
9. If you have never done anything in terms of what area pulls on your heart, could you give reasons? This will help in you refocusing yourself in terms of what will matter at the end of it all.
10. What would you do if you knew you could not fail?
11. What would you do even if nobody paid you?
12. What makes you come alive?

Passion

I want to stop here and just share about passion. Why? Because your purpose will be attached to what you are passionate about and it is that passion that will fuel your vision and your mission. We have all been created to be passionate about some things, in those things, we also seem to have an insatiable passion for one thing in particular. This one thing that you feel very strongly about, this one thing that if money was not an issue and you have all the money you need in life, you will dedicate your life totally to seeing that thing change, transform and impact others, is your passion.

This is what I mean about passion. It is what drives your ability to discover and develop your God-given purpose, it is what makes you wake up daily excited and ready to conquer your world, it is your driving force.

The dictionary defines passion as a very powerful feeling. An extreme interest in or wish for doing something.

Matthew 6:21 says: *"For where your treasure is, there your heart will be also."*

Your passion can be your treasure when you put in the totality of your being. You do not need to be inspired or motivated when you have a true passion for something or a cause. You are generally self-motivated and inspired if you have a strong conviction about a thing; you will pay whatever price, go to whatever length to get it done as you have pictured it in your mind.

Passion is what drives us to be better and more creative. The energy we possess when we are doing something we feel passionate about is incredible. When you are doing something passionately, it becomes easier to accomplish every following step.

At 50 please, you must have a passion for something, a cause you will dedicate the rest of your life to pursue and impact with. We have been created to be a solution to a problem, to bring deliverance to a generation, to ease the burden of a passion, part of God's DNA in us is passion. I am passionate about women. I believe with all my heart that I am called to teach, train and facilitate transformation for women from every nation, it has been a passion in me for at least over 20 years of my life. I have grown and developed more in it and God has been transitioning me in different realms of this passion to see me continue to grow that passion. I am convinced for the rest of my life that this passion cannot die, that's why I have a mentoring academy for women and a birthing centre, not to birth physical children but I'm anointed to help women pregnant with the purposes of God birth those ministries and initiatives.

I can do this without been paid even though I have attached a seed as an exchange to the ministry but even if no one pays me, I have enough passion in me to do it daily. As a matter of fact, I do it daily both in a structural manner and not. Anyone who knows me will testify that Ruth Mateola is passionate about women discovering, developing and deploying their God-given potential. I hate to see women reduced to baby mamas and kitchen gurus; there is more to your life as a woman than being someone's wife or mother. God has loaded the woman just as he loaded the man to multiply, subdue, have dominion, and make impact. I have a passion to see women fulfil that mandate.

I know I have asked you earlier what you are passionate about. I need you to go more deeper in this and begin to pray to God if you do not have a solid passion for a cause yet, for God to begin to put a passion in your heart that can lead

48

you to building a godly legacy for your children and the next generation. Believe me, it is possible and God needs you.

People who make a difference in their own lives and the world do so by following their passion. This means making the conscious decision to give up other enjoyable activities to focus your energy on the most important activities. Doing what you love is very hard work yet rewarding at the same time. The good news is that when you pursue your passion, you'll not only like where you end up, but enjoy the journey along the way.

Look at your life and highlight the things you love that you are willing to suffer for. This self-reflection will give you insight into what you are passionate about. If you are not sure, just pick something you enjoy and see if you're willing to give up other activities to spend more time on it. Remember that in life you can choose and change your actions—just also keep in mind that you're responsible for the consequences.

Don't settle for a life that is only so-so.

Start living your best life today.

What Did You Want to Be as a Kid?

Do you remember those days when the world was a perfect place for living? When there was nothing to worry about? When the only thing that occupied your attention was how to have fun? Those were great times! Many of us would like to go back to those wonderful times.

Remember what you wanted to be as a kid. **Where are you today**? Have you accomplished any of those past wishes? I am pretty sure you're now doing something completely different, which is not interesting at all, and it is so far away from the things you have fantasised about as a kid.

Write down your childhood ideas. Don't worry, it can be one idea, five or even ten ideas, who knows? Write them all.

What Are You Constantly Talking to Your Friends About?

When we learn something new, regarding the area we feel passionate about, we can't wait to tell it to our friends. Regardless of the fact that they might be interested in it or not, if they are really close to us, and we would want to share the things that are important to us with them.

It is time you start listening to what you're saying to your friends. You should charge them to remember and write down the things you are constantly babbling about. It doesn't matter if it's about diet, clothings, cars, sports or something else. The thing you're constantly talking about, and never get tired of, is something you feel passionate about.

Write down the things you are constantly talking about.

What Would You Do if Everything Could Be Unlimited?

It is hard to imagine, but you are in a situation of having limitless supplies of money, food, drink, and everything else you need for living. The question is, **how will you spend your day**?

This is a hard question for the people who are not aware of their passions. But that is why we have had the first two questions, so that we could now give some smart ideas for this one, more easily. You need to give at least three answers to this question. It does not matter if your answers will be activities or things. The important thing is to find the idea of how you would like to spend that perfect day.

This is where the thinking starts. **Search for that thing or activity** that comes up the most for you and write it down. Note that it does not necessarily have to be only one activity. In fact, most people usually feel passionate about more than one thing in life.

Conclusion

To live your passion means to live your life to the fullest. Everything else is a mere waste of time. It is time for you to find your passion if you have not yet done that.

To find your passion, you need to put yourself in some extreme situations. The situation where you are putting yourself into a world where everything is unlimited, or where you have only a few more hours left to live may be the best solution for finding your passion.

Do not waste another minute of your life! If you are not living your passion, you can hardly say that you are living a great life. Things are simple; money is not the measure of success—happiness and passion are.

— ❧ —

Since you have identified hopefully some things or something that you are passionate about, I want you to begin the journey of developing that passion. Write here what you believe you need to develop it.

Mentorship

One of the things you will need in supporting you to understand, develop and deploy this passion is MENTORSHIP.

John Crosby said, "Mentoring is a brain to pick, an ear to listen, and a push in the right direction."

You need someone who has reached a destination to help you to reach yours. I have noticed that in our world today, many do not want to pay the price to be mentored or coached. For every Joshua, there was a Moses; for every Esther, there was a Mordecai. You need someone to show you the way, to counsel you, to teach you, to train you, to support and love you, to help and balance you.

Mentoring is a system of semi-structured guidance whereby one person shares their knowledge, skills, and experiences to assist others to progress in their own lives and careers. Mentors need to be readily accessible and prepared to offer help as the need arises—within agreed bounds.

Mentoring is more than "giving advice" or passing on what your experience was in an area or situation. It's about motivating and empowering the other person to identify their own issues and goals, and helping them to find ways of resolving or reaching them—not by doing it for them, or expecting them to "do it the way I did it", but by understanding and respecting different ways of working.

The role of a mentor:
- Manage the relationship
- Encourage
- Nurture
- Teach
- Offer mutual respect
- Respond to the learner's needs

Do you have a Mentor?
If you do not have a mentor, it is time to get one. Prayerfully ask the Lord to lead you to finding a mentor. Being part of a mentoring academy where you can grow and thrive with others is key to your development and your jubilee season.

Reflection:
Take time to reflect on this chapter and write out your thoughts and instructions from the Lord.

"*The greatest wealth is health.*"

- Ruth Mateola

Chapter 4

Health in Jubilee

"Good health is not something we can buy. However, it can be an extremely valuable savings account."

– Anne Wilson Schaef

HEALTH IS wealth. No matter how rich you are, if your health fails you, everything else has failed you. I used to be able to eat anything I like whenever I like, however I liked it but turning 50 has given me a huge wake up call to my health and I'm going to be looking at both physical, mental and emotional health.

I grew up being very skinny, a size 8 to be precise and I loved my body and used to flaunt it. Fast forward to getting married and being pregnant with my first son, I went from a size 8/10 to a whopping size 20/22. Believe me, I cannot really say how I arrived there but I can remember the change in my appetite and the love of unhealthy food that attached itself to me during pregnancy and childbirth. I did not pay any attention to my body and before I could take charge and start working on it, I found out I was pregnant again, and this was where it plateaued for many years.

I lost total control of myself. I kept eating without having any knowledge about what to eat, when to eat and how to eat—I just ate on demand. The damage did not come to light until the year 2006 while we were living in America and I became very fat and uncomfortable. I was managing to fit into a size 22 outfit. I was desperate, yet I did not know what to do or how to do it, I began to pray about it. I began to pray because I was honestly at my wit's end and my husband who had never had to lose a pound in his life was adding to the pressure for me to lose weight and get back to being healthy.

The Lord spoke to me clearly from 1 Corinthians 6:18-20 where it says our bodies does not belong to us, we have been purchased with the priceless blood of Christ and so we must glorify God with our body and spirit which are both God's. What an awakening. The conviction was strong and I could not shake it off, so I began to investigate food. What is food? Why should we eat it? How should we eat it? When should we eat it? There was a friend of mine who started eating raw foods at the time and I knew I could not do raw foods so I continued to research and the first thing that hit me was in Leviticus 23 where God specified the clean foods to eat and the foods not to eat and I was amazed to see that God who knows all things had pre-planned good food for us, we are the ones self-sabotaging with all our mixes and matches that we do with food.

I went on a brand-new journey of cleaning out the rubbish so that I could put in new food and I won this battle. I went from a size 22 to a size 10. I even wrote a book about my journey titled, *A Style for Living, A Clarion Call to Health and Total Wellness*. On this journey, I discovered that health is more than just dieting. It is about looking after every area of your wellness and being intentional about your choices and actions.

I went as far as going to educate myself in nutrition and got a certification as a wellness coach whereby I started teaching people how to look after their health and wellbeing.

Fast forward now to 2020, too many people are dying unnecessarily due to poor health. We have taken our bodies for granted for so long that people are just dropping like flies, diseases that were never rampant in the generation of our mothers are now killing young people in the prime of their lives. This is due to a lack of discipline and loss of value in taking care of our health. You see, you can catch a flu, cold etc. but you don't catch cancer, or diabetes, or high blood pressure—these are diseases that are developed over time and our food choices contribute to the development and danger of these diseases. Please do not wait till your jubilee to start taking care of yourself—that is my main message for this chapter. I therefore, want to charge and implore you to start taking care of yourself now!

You have to realise that a great price truly has been paid for your life and your body which is God's temple and you must honour God by taking good care of the gift he has given you. You cannot continue to put trash inside your body and expect to be healthy. Do you know that your body is the vehicle that will carry you to your destination in life and help you to fulfil your purpose? Therefore, if you want to get to your destination you must pay real attention to your vehicle.

Make it a lifestyle to look after yourself, do not get too busy with life that you forget to do due diligence on your health. We live in a generation where so many young people are dying due to terrible diseases and I believe we can play our own part in doing the right things and then trust God for the rest. First, you must educate yourself and then invest that knowledge back into a healthy and wholesome life.

Never forget that you are what you eat, and changes should not be made just because you want to look good and pretty but because you want to live well and live long to enjoy and fulfil your God-given purpose. There are the types of food group:

Carbohydrates are the sugars, starches and fibres found in fruits, grains, vegetables, and milk products. The American Diabetes Association notes that **carbohydrates** are the body's main source of energy. They are called **carbohydrates** because, at the chemical level, they contain carbon, hydrogen, and oxygen.

Carbohydrates are primarily used as a fuel source and they provide us with the energy our brains and bodies need to function. There are two types of carbohydrates - simple and complex carbohydrates. Complex carbohydrates provide more sustained energy and are found in wholegrain pasta and bread, while simple carbohydrates can cause your blood sugar levels to spike; they are found in sweets, cakes and biscuits.

Complex carbohydrates are often high in fibre and packed with vitamins and minerals. This type of carbohydrate is harder to break down and foods such as brown rice and oatmeal do not turn into fat as easily as simple carbohydrates that are found in fizzy drinks, crisps, and chocolate. It is, therefore, better to opt for complex carbohydrates that help us hit the recommended amount of fibre which is 30 grams a day.

As Africans, we do not pay any attention to the level of carbohydrates that we consume as a nation. Most of our favourite foods are loaded with carbohydrates which once eaten turns into sugar that increases our chance of obesity and other cardiovascular diseases. Therefore, as you grow older you certainly need to lower your intake of carbohydrates. It should not be the highest on your plate, rather, it should be the lowest.

I have met many people who comfort themselves by saying they do not like vegetables or fruits; they must eat all these foods that impacts their bodies negatively. On my journey to health, I discovered you can retrain your taste buds. You can change from being a sweet tooth to a non-sweet tooth, it is all about re-educating your mind and attaching value to long life and great health. The things you never thought can taste good will begin to taste good.

The white rice, sugar, chocolates, starchy foods, and sodas must be drastically reduced out of your diet by 50. Introducing intermittent fasting that gives opportunity for your system to rest is also very good.

Drinking loads of water to clean out your system is also important and refreshing—all these changes make a huge difference.

List here the different types of carbohydrate foods you eat and how often you eat them.
Changes can only come when we can identify and acknowledge what is being done wrong. Now, I want you to write how you cook these carbohydrates and what you eat them with. I won't give you an example because I want you to be honest here. I know how I used to eat carbohydrates and believe me; it was deadly.

The body uses fat as a fuel source, and fat is the major storage form of energy in the body. Fat also has many other important functions in the body, and a moderate amount is needed in the diet for good health. Fats in food come in several forms, including saturated, monounsaturated, and polyunsaturated. Too much fat or too much of the wrong type of fat can be unhealthy.

Some examples of foods that contain fats are butter, oil, nuts, meat, fish, and some dairy products.

Saturated fats

We recommend these healthy choices:

- Coconut oil for its many health benefits
- MCT oil
- Raw butter

For people who eat meat: consume grass fed meat only. Processed meats that contain saturated fats like bacon, hot dogs, sausages, and lunch meats should not be eaten as they are class 1 carcinogens.

Monounsaturated fats

Monounsaturated fats protect the heart and support insulin sensitivity, fat storage, weight loss, and healthy energy levels. Healthy choices include:

- Avocado
- Macadamia nuts
- Olives and olive oil

Less healthy choices:

- Canola oil (unless its organic, canola oil is made from GMOs and is highly processed and refined).
- Peanuts – they tend to be high in moulds, which produce aflatoxin, a toxin known to cause cancer. Peanuts also cause inflammation and are highly allergenic.

61

Polyunsaturated fats

- Polyunsaturated fats include Omega 3 and Omega 6 fats. Omega 3 fats reduce inflammation and support healthy hormone levels and cell membranes. Omega 6 fatty acids are important to support healthy brain and muscle functions but on the downside, they promote inflammation in the body.
- We only need a small amount of omega 6 fatty acids in our diet, yet the standard American diet is filled with them (e.g. most baked goods, packaged foods like cookies and crackers, chips, French fries, breads, and snacks). Corn, soybean, safflower, cottonseed, grapeseed, and sunflower oils are all high in omega 6 fats and are not stable. This means any food that is fried, baked, or microwaved using these oils will oxidize and create an inflammatory response in the body.

Trans fats

This is the worst type of fat. *It is a by-product of a process called hydrogenation that is used to turn healthy oils into solids and to prevent them from becoming rancid. When vegetable oil is heated in the presence of hydrogen and a heavy-metal catalyst such as palladium and hydrogen atoms are added to the carbon chain, this turns oils into solids. It also makes healthy vegetable oils more like not-so-healthy saturated fats. On the food label ingredient list, this manufactured substance is typically listed as "partially hydrogenated oil". This is a killer for our African way of cooking where we clog up our organs with this bad oil.*

Corn and soy oils are high in omega 6 which most already get enough of in their diets. Too much omega 6 leads to an inflammatory response in the body. This kind of dietary inflammation is the root cause of most chronic diseases including heart disease, the number one killer. Quite simply, the best choice for your health is to incorporate clean fats and the least processed fats. Always eat organic foods.

- Cold pressed flax oil (never heated)
- Coconut oil (can safely heat)
- MCT oil
- Olive oil
- Raw butter
- Ghee butter for high heat cooking
- Avocado
- Raw cacao butter
- Grass fed pastured meats, dairy and eggs
- Raw nuts
- Sustainably sourced salmon, sardines, krill oil

Sugar

Chances are that you already know that eating too much sugar isn't good for you yet you are probably still overdoing it. Americans eat an average of about 270 calories of sugar each day, that's about 17 teaspoons a day, compared to the recommended limits of about 12 teaspoon per day or 200 calories.

Sugary drinks, candy, baked goods, and sweetened dairy are the main sources of added sugar but even savoury foods, like breads, tomato sauce, and protein bars, can have sugar, making it all too easy to end up with a surplus of the sweet stuff. To complicate it further, added sugars can be hard to spot on nutrition labels since they can be listed under several names, such as corn syrup, agave nectar, palm sugar, cane juice, or sucrose.

No matter what it is called, sugar is sugar, and when in excess, it can negatively affect your body in many ways. Here is a closer look at how sugar can mess with your health, from head to toe.

Your Brain

Eating sugar gives your brain a huge surge of a feel-good chemical called dopamine, which explains why you are more likely to crave a candy bar at 3 p.m. than an apple or a carrot. This is because whole foods like fruits and veggies don't cause the brain to release as much dopamine. If you keep doing this, your brain starts to need more and more sugar to get that same feeling of pleasure. This causes those "gotta-have-it" feelings for your after-dinner ice cream that are so hard to tame.

Your Mood

The occasional candy or cookie can give you a quick burst of energy (or "sugar high") by raising your blood sugar levels fast. When your levels drop as your cells absorb the sugar, you may feel jittery and anxious (a.k.a. the dreaded "sugar crash"). But if you're reaching into the candy jar too often, sugar starts to have an effect on your mood beyond that 3 p.m. splurge. Studies have linked a high sugar intake to a greater risk of depression in adults.

Your Skin

Another side effect of inflammation is that it may make your skin age faster. Excess sugar attaches to proteins in your bloodstream and creates harmful molecules called "AGEs" or Advanced Glycation End products.

These molecules do exactly what they sound like they do: age your skin. They have been shown to damage collagen and elastin in your skin—protein fibres that keep your skin firm and youthful. The result? Wrinkles and saggy skin.

Your Liver

An abundance of added sugar likely contains fructose or high fructose corn syrup. Fructose is processed in the liver and when it is taken in large amounts, it can damage the liver. When fructose is broken down in the liver, it is transformed into fat. In turn, this causes:

- Non-alcoholic fatty liver disease (NAFLD): This is seen as excess fat build-up in the liver.
- Non-alcoholic steatohepatitis (NASH): This is a fatty liver, inflammation and "steatosis" which is scarring of the liver.

Scarring eventually cuts off blood supply to the liver. Many of these develop into cirrhosis and will need a liver transplant.

Your Heart

When you eat excess sugar, the extra insulin in your bloodstream can affect your arteries. It causes their walls to get inflamed, grow thicker than normal and stiffer, this stresses your heart and damages it over time. This can lead to heart diseases like heart failure, heart attacks, and strokes. Research also suggests that eating less sugar can help to lower blood pressure, a major risk factor for heart disease. People who eat a lot of added sugar (where at least 25% of their calories comes from added sugar) are twice as likely to die of heart disease than those whose diets include less than 10% of total calories from added sugar.

Your Pancreas

When you eat, your pancreas pumps out insulin. But if you are eating way too much sugar and your body stops responding properly to insulin, your pancreas starts pumping out even more insulin. Eventually, your overworked pancreas will break down and your blood sugar levels will rise, setting you up for type 2 diabetes and heart disease.

Your Kidneys

If you have diabetes, too much sugar can lead to kidney damage. The kidneys play an important role in filtering your blood. Once blood sugar levels reach a certain amount, the kidneys start to release excess sugar into your urine. If left uncontrolled, diabetes can damage the kidneys, which prevents them from doing their job in filtering out waste in your blood. This can lead to kidney failure.

Your Body Weight

This probably is not news to you—the more sugar you eat, the more you will weigh. Research shows that people who drink sugar-sweetened beverages tend to weigh more—and be at higher risk for type 2 diabetes—than those who don't. One study even found that people who increased their sugar intake gained about 1.7 pounds in less than 2 months. Excess amounts of sugar can inflame fat cells causing them to release chemicals that increase weight.

Unbalanced ways of eating any of the above is a contributor to some diseases that are silent killers. I want you now to begin to consider how you have handled these different types of food in your life till now. Have you bothered to pay any attention? If you have not, this is the time to start. Recognise you cannot eat everything you want whenever you want even if you are a size '0'.

A great myth that many has believed is that just because they are not fat means they are healthy. Many people that I know of who have died of certain diseases were not more than a size 10/12, so because you are not fat does not mean you are healthy. It is about understanding your body. How does it work and what food will work well for your body type? It is about valuing the gift you have been given and treating it well enough to show your love and value for the one who gave it to you.

It is about stopping your busy life to begin to pay good attention to yourself before it is too late. We must never allow disaster to be what jerks us up to begin to do the right thing about our health. I have been up and down with mine, but at a few months to 50, as I am writing this book, I have once and for all, taken back the control of my health.

I came to a conclusion again, that my life is worth it, that I have a lot to accomplish for God, and that He has played his own part and I need to play mine—just as the bible says, obedience is better than sacrifice. I have decided I want to feel good and look amazingly good. I am making it a lifestyle, this is not a quick fix diet to look good for my jubilee celebration, but it is to look good till the day the Lord calls me home, to pay a price now so that I can play more later.

So, whether you are still yet to be 50 or some have crossed the 50 mark, start taking your health extremely seriously from TODAY. Please let me say here that the reason I started with food is because it makes up for about 85% of our health, exercise is less than 10% of what makes us healthy. You must first take charge of what goes into your mouth before you can start strengthening yourself.

Exercise

What is exercise? Exercise is any bodily activity that enhances or maintains physical fitness and overall health and wellness. Exercise and physical activity fall into four basic categories—endurance, strength, balance, and flexibility. Most people tend to focus on one activity or type of exercise and think they are doing enough. Each type is different. Doing them all will give you more benefits. Mixing it up also helps to reduce boredom and cut your risk of injury.

Endurance

Endurance, or aerobic activities increases your breathing and heart rate. They keep your heart, lungs, and circulatory system healthy and improve your overall fitness. Building your endurance level makes it easier to carry out many of your everyday activities. Endurance exercises include:

- Brisk walking or jogging
- Yard work (mowing, raking, digging)
- Dancing

Strength

Strength exercises make your muscles stronger. They may help you stay independent and carry out everyday activities, such as climbing stairs and carrying groceries. These exercises also are called "strength training" or "resistance training". Strength exercises include:

- Lifting weights
- Using a resistance band
- Using your own body weight

Balance

Balance exercises help to prevent falls, a common problem in older adults. Many lower-body strength exercises will also improve your balance. Balance exercises include:

- Standing on one foot
- Heel-to-toe walk
- Tai Chi

Flexibility

Flexibility exercises stretch your muscles and can help your body stay limber. Being flexible gives you more freedom of movement for other exercises as well as for your everyday activities, including driving and getting dressed. Flexibility exercises include:

- Shoulder and upper arm stretch
- Calf stretch

To stay healthy, adults should try to be active every day and aim to achieve at least 150 minutes of physical activity over a week through a variety of activities.

For most people, the easiest way to get moving is to make activities a part of everyday life, like walking or cycling instead of using the car to get around. However, the more you do, the better, and taking part in activities such as sports and exercise will make you even healthier.

For any type of activity to benefit your health, you need to be moving quick enough to raise your heart rate, breathe faster and feel warmer. This level of effort is called moderate intensity activity. If you are working at a moderate intensity, you should still be able to talk but you won't be able to sing the words to a song.

It is medically proven that people who do regular physical activities have:

- up to a 35% lower risk of coronary heart disease and stroke
- up to a 50% lower risk of type 2 diabetes
- up to a 50% lower risk of colon cancer
- up to a 20% lower risk of breast cancer
- a 30% lower risk of early death
- up to an 83% lower risk of osteoarthritis
- up to a 68% lower risk of hip fracture
- a 30% lower risk of falls (among older adults)
- up to a 30% lower risk of depression
- up to a 30% lower risk of dementia

People are less active nowadays, partly because technology has made our lives easier. We drive cars or take public transport. Machines wash our clothes.

We entertain ourselves in front of a TV or computer screen. Fewer people are doing manual work, and most of us have jobs that involve little physical effort. Work, household chores, shopping and other necessary activities are far less demanding than for previous generations.

We move around less and burn off less energy than people used to. Research suggests that many adults spend more than seven (7) hours a day sitting down, at work, on transport or in their leisure time.

People aged over 65 spend ten (10) hours or more each day sitting or lying down, making them the most sedentary age group.

Inactivity is described by the Department of Health as a "silent killer". Evidence is emerging that sedentary behaviour, such as sitting or lying down for long periods, is bad for your health. Not only should you try to raise your activity levels, but you should also reduce the amount of time you and your family spend sitting down.

Common examples of sedentary behaviour include watching TV, using a computer, using the car for short journeys, and sitting down to read, talk or listen to music. This type of behaviour is thought to increase your risk of developing many chronic diseases, such as heart disease, stroke and type 2 diabetes, as well as weight gain and obesity.

Benefits of Exercising
- Exercise increases energy levels
- Exercise improves muscle strength
- Exercise can help you to maintain a healthy weight
- Exercise improves brain function
- Exercise is good for your heart
- Regular exercise lowers your risk of developing type 2 diabetes
- Exercise enhances your immune system
- Staying active reduces the likelihood of developing some degenerative bone diseases

- Exercise may help to reduce the risk of certain cancers
- Active people tend to sleep better
- Exercise improves your mood and gives you an improved sense of well-being
- Exercise can help prevent and treat mental illnesses like depression
- Keeping fit can reduce some of the effects of aging.

Do you have any exercise routine in your life? If yes, what kind of exercise(s) do you do? If no, you should put a plan together now!

High blood pressure

As a general guide: ideal blood pressure is between 90/60mmHg and 120/80mmHg. High blood pressure is 140/90mmHg or higher. Low blood pressure is 90/60mmHg or lower.

When was the last time you checked your blood pressure? What was your reading?
When was the last time you had a full check-up done? What were your results?

I am not going to give you all the information. I want you to go ahead and do this personal exercise for yourself. Answer all the questions below, take the time out to go and get the answers for yourself.

1. **What is your BMI? (BMI an approximate measure of whether someone is over or underweight, calculated by dividing their weight in kilograms by the square of their height in metres). I need you to go and find out what your BMI is.**

   Having an annual health check is very important, many who have done this consistently have been lucky to have early intervention and care. This is done by health professionals at your local GP surgery, often by a nurse or healthcare assistant who will ask you some questions about your lifestyle and family history, measure your weight, and height, and take your blood pressure and blood test. Your blood test results can show your chances of getting heart diseases, stroke, kidney diseases and diabetes.

2. **What is your lifestyle like? I want you to really think about how you have been living and eating, including your daily routines so we can see how this can impact your health.**

3. **Do you know of any family history you have identified?**

———————————— ❦ ————————————

4. What is your height and weight? Write it down, then do a research as to whether you are in good shape or not.
5. How is your eyesight? Have you ever had it tested?
6. Do you do frequent dental appointments? It may sound silly, but a lot of people have not been to the dentist in years.

———————————————————————————————

By 50, you should have developed a health routine for yourself that includes:

- Eating right
- Exercise
- Supplements
- Annual check ups

Reflection:
Take this time to reflect on this chapter and write out your thoughts and instructions from the Lord.

"Don't buy things you can't afford with money you don't have to impress people you don't like."

\- Dave Ramsey

Chapter 5

Finance in Jubilee

"Honour the LORD with your wealth and with the first fruits of all your produce; then your barns will be filled with plenty, and your vats will be bursting with wine." (Proverbs 3:9–10 NKJV)

ACCORDING TO the Bible, money answers everything. I have come to believe it to a very great extent. Yes, there are certain things in life that money cannot buy, but having money makes your life easy and enjoyable—most especially when you are coming into your fifties. If the truth be told, this is an extremely sensitive topic for us all. For some, they have managed to plan financially; for others they have not. My focus here is for those who have not planned and unfortunately, a lot of people fall into this category. My husband defines money as a reward you get for solving problems; he says the amount you get paid is determined by the level of problem you are solving. For example, the CEO gets a different level of reward than the cleaner simply because of the level of problem they are solving.

I have discovered a few categories of people when it comes to planning financially for the future.

- Those who work jobs all their lives and not really the jobs they like because they did not get an education and did not build a good career, so they just do odds jobs for survival.
- Those who build a career but then it was not lucrative enough—believe me there are some jobs that the take home is not worth going out for, but people have to do them because the service needs to be provided.
- Those who found out the lucrative careers, studied and built good income through it.

Let me say here that it is never too late to learn something new and build yourself financially for your later years. I know there are so many schemes around e.g.

- ISA
- Bonds
- Stocks/Shares
- Mutual Funds

I will encourage you to investigate and find which works best for you. But now let's even ask where you are at, life has happened to many of us, it might not have played out how you envisaged it and it might have had a huge effect on your finances, but please try to seal the leak and start building for your future.

I did a survey a few years ago and I was horrified to see that many do not have a saving culture. We spend all that we earn, and this happens due to a lack of proper planning for different seasons of life. We spend as we earn, we live from one paycheck to another leaving nothing behind that can be saved. The last thing on many people's mind is saving because they are still struggling for daily survival. However, if you do not acquire a saving culture, the other seasons of life may not be better.

Many spend money on too many perishable things that has resulted in overwhelming debt. When I came into the UK in the 90s, even with the little we made then, I saved money. As a single person, I learnt to live within my means, and I was able to save a lot of my income and still have a decent life.

After getting married, I don't know what happened to me, but I stopped saving and incurred debts. I thank God that my husband had a good saving culture due to his upbringing and was able to plan for and maintain our family finances. Despite his ability to save, we still got into debt and for a season, we were robbing Peter to pay Paul. We were neck deep in debt but by the grace of God, we were able to still secure some investment properties and new savings. We had to trust God to help us get out of debt by teaching us biblical principles that saved us and also by educating ourselves about our finances and being disciplined enough to implement the knowledge we acquired.

We lived in America for a season in life and all I did was

develop myself in a new career such that when we came back to the UK, it helped us to settle down as a family because I was able to work and earn a decent living for us to begin our new season. I have to say here, that we kept on saving as a family, I had to remind myself of my family goals daily and constantly to support my saving culture, so I don't fall off the wagon.

I was confronted by something that was taking my finances that the Holy Spirit convicted me about. It is called "Aso Ebi"—those from an African origin will understand this. I believe this needs to be eradicated from our culture because many have lost good savings due to a culture of always buying new outfits for every occasion.

The money that we spend on this unnecessary stuff can add up to cause chaos in our finances if we are not careful and that is money that could have been saved for a better future use. I had to learn to begin to say NO to some things, especially when I got into my mid-40s, I realised that I needed to start some serious saving. My husband and I decided to enrol our children in private schools and I have to tell you that it has taken a great chunk of our income, but we know that it is a good investment for the future of our children. There was a season where we could not save as much as we would have loved to but because we had seasons of big returns from former investments, it kept yielding and we kept reinvesting and God has been really faithful to us.

We are both soon turning 50, our first two children will

be graduates by the time my hubby turns 50 next year, so we are left with our 14-year-old. We are now saving and investing more for our future.

1. What has been your own spending pattern? Please be very descriptive while identifying the things you spend money on mostly.
2. Are you a saver? If no, why not? Can you identify your belief system when it comes to money and saving?
3. If yes, what is your saving culture? How do you save? When do you save? What percentage do you save?
4. Do you earn enough right now to begin to save for your future?
5. Have you thought about what you can do to increase your earning ability? Are you maximising your capacity to solve big problems so you can be rewarded with a better renumeration? If not, start thinking of what you can do.

Please do not wait till your 50s to start saving. I am a firm believer that things practised over time becomes a lifestyle. You must learn to save and invest for your tomorrow as your lifestyle. You need to make living within your means a lifestyle by eliminating unnecessary expenditures.

81

❧

What unnecessary spending must you eliminate? List them and try to write how much money you spend on these things—it can be as little as Starbucks coffee daily. All these things add up to deprive you of saving eventually.

Debt

"The rich rules over the poor, and the borrower is the slave of the lender." (Proverbs 22:7 NKJV)

"Financial peace isn't the acquisition of stuff. It's learning to live on less than you make, so you can give money back and have money to invest." – Dave Ramsey

One of the greatest evils of a great financial future is DEBT. This is a silent killer that hinders us from having and enjoying the life that Christ died for us to enjoy. Many of God's children are stuck today because of the chains of debt. Many people owe so much that that debt has enslaved them.

Debt can happen in different ways which include:
- Unforeseen circumstances
- Living beyond your means
- Lack of delayed gratification
- Lack of enough income
- Overstretching standard of living.

Whichever category you fall into, I want you to know debt is a killer. You must try your best now and begin to eliminate it out of your life. Is it possible to live debt free? My answer is that you absolutely can. You first need to know that your credit cards and overdrafts are not an extension of your income, start this by cutting your coat according to your size. If you are currently in debt, the first thing to do is to STOP your spending.

You must know what to spend and what not to spend, we are living in a world where delayed gratification is no longer the order of the day.

Many people want it NOW AND TODAY. Even if you can afford it, it does not necessarily mean you need it or must have it. I have seen many in their fifties struggling financially due to incredible level of debt. Marriages break up many times because of the contribution of financial debt; this is a serious thing and as I am turning 50, I am rethinking my financial future and thanking God that I have eliminated all debts in my life. Now, I do not have the extra burden of being weighed down by debt.

We also come from a culture of self-deception where everyone wants to copy others without being able to afford what those you are trying to copy can afford.

Ask yourself for a minute, who is guiding your financial decisions on a daily basis? Is it your genuine needs or your unnecessary wants?

Stop here for a minute and tell me, do you have any
debt? How did you get into debt? What happened?
What have you done or plan to do with these debts?
Are you increasing it or ignoring it?

Getting out of debt is an important component of financial
planning because the high interest you pay on certain debts
can prevent you from saving money for the future or investing.
Establishing and implementing a debt repayment plan takes
discipline, but it is possible. The right repayment plan for you
depends on the amount and number of debts you owe. If you
have a lot of high-interest debts, for example, list all the debts
in order from highest to lowest interest rates. Pay any extra
money you have toward the first debt. Once you have repaid it,
move onto the next debt—repeat this process until you have
repaid all your debts. If you have too many debts, consider
paying off the one with the smallest balance first and then
move on to those with larger balances.

List your debts identifying the different interest rates
attached to them.

You may need to drastically cut your spending and increase

your earnings in order to pay the debt off more quickly. Once you are out of debt, reduce or even eliminate the use of credit cards to avoid going into debt again. When you do use your cards, pay the monthly statement balance in full within the grace period to avoid incurring interests. Once you have listed all your debts, you know what to do. You can no longer ignore your debts hoping they will go away, they will not. You need to get the courage to call them and start negotiating with them.

Remember, to begin to make new steps, you need to stop the old ones. You need to know what the contractual repayments are.

Here are some next steps:
Clear the smallest debts first. This will motivate you along the debt clearance
- path to keep up with the contractual repayments.
- Channel all additional income to clear smallest debts first.
- Clear the most expensive debts first.

Financial Planning

I think my biggest message in this section is to plan for your financial future now so that you do not have to struggle tomorrow. That is the essence of financial planning.

A financial plan is used to organise how you handle your money and finances, so you have less stress and are on the path to long-term success. Think of it as your roadmap or your building blocks to what is happening with your finances and what goals you aim to achieve. The benefits of having a plan include helping you save money, helping your net worth grow, and keeping you financially organised.

Here are a few things to know about financial planning for your future:

Know What You are Saving For

As the author of the *7 Habits of Highly Effective People* puts it, "begin with the end in mind". The ultimate goal of saving is to reach financial independence, where you no longer need to work to live comfortably and safely and can spend your time however you like. Have some fun and daydream about what you would do with all that free time. Add in some shorter-term goals along the way like becoming debt free or buying a new car or home. Finally, writing them down makes them more likely to happen.

Make Sure Your Saving Goals Are SMART

Once you get past the daydreaming phase, you'll want your goals to be more concrete. They should be specific, measurable, achievable, realistic, and trackable. For each goal, estimate what it will cost and how much you would need to save each month to achieve them.

How much do you think you will need on a monthly basis in your future? Has this ever occurred to you? And once you know this, how can you begin to plan for it? What do you need to do?

Find Ways to Reduce Your Expenses

Unless you have ways of earning additional income, this is where the money will come from to fund your goals. The first step is to look at your bank and credit card statements to see where your money is going. Then, get rid of anything unnecessary or wasteful that you can eliminate or replace. Some examples would be a gym membership you don't use or can replace by exercising at home or outdoors, a subscription that you don't need or can access online, cable channels that you don't watch, a cell phone that can be replaced with a cheaper plan, coffee and lunch that you can bring from home instead of buying out. Finally, see if you can reduce your remaining bills by shopping around or negotiating them down.

Create a Budget

Yes, the dreaded "b" word. Instead of looking at it as deprivation, think of budgeting as making sure your spending reflects your priorities and values. After all, we are bombarded every day by marketing and advertising designed by some of the smartest people on Madison Avenue to convince us that their priorities are ours. Budgeting allows you to take back control over your money and make sure that your needs (both short and long term) are being fulfilled before your wants. If necessary, that means weighing each of your remaining expenses against your saving goals and making the conscious decision of what takes priority.

A budget is an estimate or outline of income and expenditure over a set period. Why budget? Budget is important because it:

- Helps you gain control over your finances
- Gives you clarity into your financial position
- Helps you prioritise spending
- Helps you identify and limit waste
- Helps decrease your financial stress levels
- Helps you respond and adapt quickly to changing financial circumstances
- Supports you in achieving your financial goals

Here are some tips on budgeting:

- Have a monthly budget and break it down to a weekly budget if necessary
- Be realistic about your income and expenditure
- If income is unknown, include smallest estimates of income
- If the level of income uncertainty is high, prepare a separate worst-case scenario budget and a best-case scenario budget
- Use your most recent bank and credit card statements to estimate

- Show breakdown of expenses on a granular level
- Refer to receipts (which can be maintained electronically to limit paper-overload) to estimate expenses
- Keep important documents like rent agreements, mortgage statements etc.

List all your expenditures and your incomes.

Build an Emergency Fund

Having a financial safety net is a key component of financial planning. This is why it's important to build an emergency fund of three to six months' worth of living expenses. This financial cushion will allow you to cover unplanned expenses and leave your long-term savings and investments alone, keeping your financial plan on track.

As the name suggests, an emergency fund should only be used for real emergencies, such as a job loss or sudden medical expense. Importantly, when you dip into your emergency fund, aim to bring it back up to the full amount as quickly as possible to ensure that the funds are there when you need them again.

You can incorporate an emergency fund into your financial plan by directing as little as 2% of your take-home pay into a separate savings account from where you do your everyday banking. After six months, consider increasing that contribution by 1% to 2% every six months to one year to build the financial cushion even faster.

We can never emphasise unplanned circumstances or situations hence why it is important to have emergency funding for your family. I have witnessed many families with situations where there is a job loss for both partners and because in their day to day life there was no preparation of putting money aside that can sustain the family in the possibility of job loss or any adverse circumstances due to health or bereavement, they started having financial issues.

My pastor taught us years ago to make sure that while you are working, you put aside emergency money that can help you take care of your family for at least six months or more if anything happens.

I know we can think this is impossible because our expenditure might be so much that we do not have enough to put aside. If this is the case, I believe you need to reassess your expenditure and cut out some things out to allow you to put this fund aside. Our prayer is that you may never need to use it and it can be transferred into savings for the family which will be a better option than to not have it at all.

Have you ever had an emergency fund? If yes, how did you save it? If no, why not?

❧

Looking at your present income and expenditure, what can you eliminate to give you the opportunity to put this money aside?

Savings

Savings is the portion of income not spent on current expenditures. Because a person does not know what will happen in the future, money should be saved to pay for unexpected events or emergencies. An individual's car may breakdown, their dishwasher could begin to leak, or a medical emergency could occur. Without savings, unexpected events can become large financial burdens. Therefore, savings helps an individual or family become financially secure. Money can also be saved to purchase expensive items that are too costly to buy with monthly income. Buying a new camera, purchasing an automobile, or paying for a vacation can all be accomplished by saving a portion of your income.

To help a person to choose saving overspending money, money should not be viewed as what is remaining after current needs and wants to have been satisfied. "Pay yourself first" is a popular and very effective saving strategy that can help individuals choose saving overspending money.

Paying yourself first means to set aside a portion of money (10-20% of net income is recommended) for saving each time you are paid before spending any of the money. To successfully

91

practice the "pay yourself first" strategy, a person should set personal goals. Setting goals helps a person choose to save rather than spend money. A goal is defined as the end result of something a person intends to acquire, achieve, do, reach, or accomplish.

Financial goals are specific objectives to be accomplished through financial planning and this includes saving money. Setting goals helps an individual identify and focus on items that are most important to them and then make decisions that will help obtain those items. While in the process of setting goals, an individual should consider the trade-offs to those goals. A trade-off is giving up one thing for another. Every decision involves a trade-off. Being more financially secure in the future by saving is a trade-off to spending money in the present. If a person clearly understands what they are giving up in exchange for the benefits of saving money, then their saving goals will become more attainable and realistic.

When considering the trade-offs to achieving savings goals, an individual should examine their current spending as well. Spending may have to be adjusted in order to reach a financial goal and always remember to practice the pay yourself first strategy.

Culture of Savings
There is never going to be enough money to save. That is what you must first accept if you want to develop the habit of saving. A salary increase for most people will not necessarily

get them to save more. Your children finishing school will not get you to save more. A bigger client for your business will not get you to save more. Getting older will not enable you to save more. Paying off your mortgage and other debts will not get you to save more. All these are excuses not to start saving today.

If you are not saving with what you have today, chances are you will not save when you have more money simply because you do not have a culture of saving. One of the definitions I found describes culture, as a way of thinking, behaving, or working that exists in a society or organisation. In my own words—something done consistently becomes a habit; a habit done over and over becomes a way of life i.e. a culture.

If we look at our society, we have a spending culture as opposed to a savings culture. This is why most often; a bigger salary means more spending even though we often delude ourselves into thinking we will invest or save more when a higher income comes along. Trust me, the world is never going to run out of things you can buy. You may think you have the latest phone, and a month later another model or upgraded version of your phone will be there.

So, what is the importance of the habit and consequently the culture of saving? It helps remove the scarcity mentality. Most people do not save because they think they do not have enough money to save. They are consistently in the frame of mind of "there is not enough". A writer by the name of Eckhart

Tolle stated, "If the thought of lack has become a part of who you think you are, you will experience lack and all you will see is lack".

If you believe today that what you are earning is not enough, it will never be enough because you are focused on the wrong thing. To put this into practice, just start saving. Nothing is too small to start with. Work with whatever you have available and do not procrastinate. Do not wait to feel you can afford to save—just do it. After taking this leap of faith, you will discover you did not die because you saved. The things that are important went on—rent was paid, you covered your transport costs, you ate food, etc. This is the start of instilling confidence that you can do it and you will then find it easier to start increasing the amounts. If you have struggled with saving, you are better off starting with a small consistent amount and building on it rather than a large amount which you give up on in a month.

Another important reason to develop a savings culture is that it is the doorway to wealth creation. Remember you cannot create wealth if you are constantly thinking "there is never enough". I have met many people who want to know where to invest but they have never cultivated the discipline of putting money aside. Many of them are using the fact that they do not know where to invest as an excuse not to save.

You do not have to know precisely where to invest before you start saving. When you consistently save, even in something as straight forward as a savings account, you are more likely to start picking up ways and information about how best to utilise your savings.

Luck is what happens when preparation meets opportunity. Once you know you have money accumulating, your mind will start looking out for information. A conversation with someone may spark off a business idea. The share report in the daily papers may start becoming interesting to you and you will go out of your way to understand it. You may be motivated to team up with other people, so you do bigger investments. Once you start seeing what you are able to do, you get the incentive to keep increasing it.

A culture of saving tames the beast called "instant gratification" because you start to understand the value of money. For example, if you put some money every month into accumulating a particular share on the stock market, you keep track of information regarding that share and observe its performance, chances are you will not often spend that money without thinking about it and the opportunity cost.

If you do decide to spend, you are aware of the choice you have made. You are able to put aside this instant gratification and use money as a resource to live the life you really want. This savings culture allows you to put things into perspective. Is upgrading your car on debt today more important than being able to do the things that have value to you?

Lastly, if we develop a savings culture, our children will do the same and their children will do the same. This culture has a positive effect on not just you but generations to come.

It is an extremely important legacy you can leave. Children will do what they observe and if you have a spending culture in your family i.e. more emphasis is placed on how to spend money, then that is probably what they will do and teach their children to do. Given that the critical subject of money is not taught through formal education, consider yourself and your actions to be the school for your child. Ask yourself, what you are teaching them? Perhaps it is time to change the lesson.

I grew up in a home where we had all that we wanted and not necessarily needed. My father was an absentee father so as long as you have a receipt for whatever you wanted; money will be given to you. I am not sure whether this was out of his guilt of not really being there or not. I cannot remember being taught about savings as a child, I had a mentality of "if you have it spend it". So when I got married, I was not the good finance partner in the marriage.

My husband was and because he was also responsible in sorting out the family financially, I did not see the reason to start saving until my early 40s. Please don't do that to yourself. I am thankful that I do have a vocation that pays very good renumeration and seeing people come into this jubilee season financially unstable, with marriage breakdowns, loss of partners, just to mention a few were what prompted me into developing this culture of saving and I'm glad I got my wake up call.

I know people stuck in abusive situations because the lack of finances cannot allow them to leave. I see women humiliated because they don't have an income and they had not developed a saving culture, so now they are forced to ask their husbands for every mundane thing they need. Please if you are reading this and you are one that spends all or don't save, let this be your wake-up call.

1. Do you have savings? If yes, how did you start saving? If not, why not? Process here why you do not save.
2. What was your experience with money?
3. Do you have anything or things you believe is important to save for?
4. It may seem like a foolish or sensitive question, but what do you do with your salary? Yes, I know you pay bills what else do you do? I am asking you to do this so we can begin to see opportunities of how you can begin to save.

I know I have shared about saving but nothing works until you make your own plan for it to work. So, write here what your own plan for saving will be.

Investments
Another key financial element is investments. This is also another area that I have seen many without tangible

investments coming into their jubilee season. Investing is something that everyone should do. There are so many benefits of investing that it makes no sense not to get started.

If you want to build wealth and financial stability investing is what will get you there. Investments are something you buy or put your money into to get a profitable return.

Most people choose from four main types of investments, known as "asset classes":

- Shares – you buy a stake in a company
- Cash – the savings you put in a bank or building society account
- Property – you invest in a physical building, whether commercial or residential
- Fixed interest securities (also called bonds) – you loan your money to a company or government.

My experience not just as an individual but as a unit with my husband is both cash savings and property investment, the property investment I can categorically say has been a tremendous blessing in our lives. We accumulated properties, we saved for it and when we relocated to the USA for 9 years, our investment properties were a great source of supplement income for us and even when we came back to the UK it continued to be a great source of extra income and saving for our future.

There are many opportunities to get into property investment if you do your homework properly and have some savings that you can use to get into it so I will encourage you to please investigate some investment vehicles you can plug into and prepare for your future.

Do you have any investments? Have you ever thought of having any?
If you don't have any, can you think of some that you are interested in and can begin to research into?

Investments has some risks just like most things in life, the Bible says in Luke 14 that will a man build a house without first of all sitting down to count the cost and make sure he/she has enough to complete it? I want to use the next session to just share with you a few important things about risks in terms of investments.

Risks

No one likes to gamble with their savings, but the truth is there's no such thing as a "no-risk" investment. You're always taking on some risks when you invest, but the amount varies with different types of investment.

Money you place in secure deposits such as savings accounts risk losing value in real terms (purchasing power) over time. This is because the interest rate paid will not always keep up with (inflation). On the other hand, index-linked investments that follow the rate of inflation don't always follow market interest rates. This means that if inflation falls, you could earn less in interest than you expected.

Stock market investments might beat inflation and interest rates over time, but you run the risk that prices might be low at the time you need to sell. This could result in a poor return or, if prices are lower than when you bought, you risk losing money.

When you start investing, it is usually a good idea to spread your risk by putting your money into a number of different products and asset classes. That way, if one investment doesn't work out as you hope, you've still got others to fall back on.

When Should You Start Investing?

If you've got plenty of money in your cash savings account—enough to cover you for at least six months—and you want to see your money grow over the long term, then you should consider investing some of it. The right savings or investments for you will depend on how happy you are taking risks and on your current finances and future goals.

What is Risk Appetite?

Saving and investing involves a variety of risks, for example:
- The risk that an institution will fall (default risk)
- The risk your money will not keep up with rising prices (inflation risk)
- The risk that comes with share prices going up and down (volatility risk)

- The risk that you could have earned better returns elsewhere (interest-rate risk).

The trick is to strike a balance between these different risks. What will a good balance for you depend on?
- Your personal attitude to risk
- Your investment goals, time frame and need for returns
- Your personal circumstances—how much you can afford to lose (what is your capacity for loss)?

When put together, these make up what is called your "risk appetite". Of these three things, your capacity for loss and your investment goals are the most important.

Personal attitude to risk is hard to measure and can be changeable, what feels comfortable one day might not feel so the next day.

1. So, what is your risk appetite when it comes to money? Have you ever thought about it?
2. What is your capacity for loss of money? How much is too much to lose?
3. What is your attitude to risk? You need to identify and deal with this attitude because investment is so key when you are coming into your later years.

How to Assess Your Risk Appetite

Use the following steps to get an idea of your risk appetite.

Step 1 – Know What You Can Afford to Lose

Ask yourself what would happen if you lost some or all of the money you're putting into investments. This will depend on your circumstances and how much of your money you are investing. Think about people who depend on you financially and any other important financial commitments you need to be sure of meeting.

Step 2 – Work Out Your Goals and Timings

Your saving and investing choices will depend on your goals and timescales. The bigger your goal in relation to the assets or income you wish to invest, the greater the rate of return required to beat inflation and hit your goal.

Taking no volatility risk at all might make your goals impossible to achieve, taking too much might make you lose your investment.

Short-term goals – under five years – such as a car or a house deposit are best saved for in cash. If you have a short-term goal, your appetite for volatility risk would usually be low and cash products will be the best place to invest.

You do not want to be worrying about the state of the financial markets when you need your money to be readily accessible. However, cash savings run the risk of not keeping up with rising prices (inflation risk).

With longer-term goals, it is better to put your money into investments that have a better chance of giving you inflation-beating returns, such as shares, though they carry the risk of prices going down. A longer time frame gives your investment more time to recover if it falls in value. So, if you have a long-term goal it makes sense to be prepared to take on volatility risk for the opportunity of higher returns. However, as a long-term goal moves closer towards maturity, the risk balance should change.

For example, you might want to start moving into less volatile assets a few years before the goal date, to start "locking-in" gains, and to protect your investment against events like market falls. At any time, you might have a mixture of short-term or critical goals for which you want low volatility (such as saving up to move house), and some non-critical or long term goals for which you have a higher appetite for volatility (for example, saving into a treats fund, or saving towards retirement).

To make a good saving and investing plan, you need to take stock of where you stand financially. Assess your goals and what the future might hold and consider your experience and attitudes. Then, identify what money is available. A fact find is the process by which you gather that information so that you are ready to make your plan.

Reflection:

Take time to reflect on this chapter and write out your thoughts and instructions from the Lord.

"Starting today I need to forget whats gone, appreciate what still reamins, and look forward to whats coming next."

‑ Ruth Mateola

Chapter 6

Relationships in Jubilee

I AM PARTICULARLY passionate about this topic—relationships in your jubilee. This refers to the people who have made and will make a difference in your life as you continue to grow.

These relationships can be broken down into different units: Your immediate family, your husband, children, and your group of friends.

We do not have the privilege to choose our immediate family, we can't choose our parents or our siblings. We get to just do life with them the best way that we can. Many times those relationships have up and downs, they too go through different seasons and it can get disconnected or strained, my encouragement is for you to try your best to be at peace with all men as much as you can, to forgive as often as you can. I am a firm believer that people are our covering and they are more valuable than money.

You need your family to gather around you as you come

into this significant season called the jubilee, you don't want to do it alone, you don't want to be separated from those with which your formative years were built. I know for a fact that some immediate family relationships are very damaged, but it does not stop the fact that they can sometimes be necessary in our later years.

If your parents are still alive—I am speaking to those who are yet to be fifty now, because for some people, both parents would have been gone by the time they clock 50—you should be grateful that your parents are still alive to see you celebrate this great milestone. So, if they are alive make memories with them, take care of them, love on them and make sure you have no regrets when the Lord calls them home.

If there are any issues please find all means to sort it out, forgive them and ask God to help you forget the pain. Parents are the first and most important teachers in every child's life. The importance of family starts at birth and stays constant throughout life. As children grow into their teens and early adulthood, families can be a bedrock of support during times of change. Here are a few ways a strong family can support children:

Five Reasons Why Family is Important:
- To meet physical and emotional needs
- To model good values
- To provide protection
- To advocate for children's needs

- To offer guidance in all areas of life

If you are a parent—or are planning to start a family soon—reflecting on how to strengthen family relationships is important. You can make conscious choices to build positive family dynamics and help set your children up for a bright future.

What is a family? A family usually starts with parents and children, but also extends to aunts, uncles, grandparents, and cousins. Sometimes, we can build such close bonds with friends and neighbours that they feel like part of our family. There are many different types of families, and each family is unique. Truly, family structure is less important than the feeling of belonging.

Ultimately, family is about creating strong relationships and providing a sense of meaning and belonging. Families should be a source of unconditional love and a resource for all of us to weather life's changes and challenges. In healthy families, children can learn what it means to be a happily married woman or man, along with the qualities of a good father or mother. Most people would also agree on the importance of family in creating healthy individuals and strong communities.

Families Meet Physical and Emotional Needs
Parents provide necessities—food, clothing, and shelter—for children in their household but the importance of family does not end with physical needs. They should aim to support emotional needs as well.

In truth, humans have multiple layers of needs—and a healthy family can support them all. Families can look to a classical psychological concept called "Maslow's Hierarchy of Needs" to understand this concept more clearly. "Maslow's Hierarchy of Needs" has a pyramid organisation, with our most basic, physical needs at the bottom. We all need things like air, food, water, and sleep to survive. On the next level are needs related to feeling secure, such as resources for staying safe and healthy.

The next three levels of Maslow's pyramid all relate to our emotional needs. Families can play a significant role in helping children eventually meet these needs. For example, through daily comments and interactions, parents can help their children feel important, loved, and wanted. By giving children important responsibilities and involving them in relevant family decisions, parents help foster self-esteem and a feeling of being capable. A strong family can help members achieve the pinnacle of Maslow's pyramid—self-actualisation. A self-actualised person can express his or her deepest talents in meaningful ways and achieve his or her fullest potential.

In short, a strong family should be a source for much more than just basic items needed for life. A family should be a bedrock of encouragement, respect, and love to help every member thrive.

Family Helps Model Good Values
In today's hyper-connected world, it is easy to get over-exposed

to unhealthy ideas and images. However, a close family with strong values can help young family members avoid or resist negative influences. Without strong family values, young people can succumb to peer pressure and stumble upon unwanted consequences, including substance abuse and various forms of addiction. It is best to start embodying good values when your kids are young. That way, as your children encounter critical decisions, they are already prepared to make good choices.

In children's earliest years, they look to parents as role models. If you show them positive behaviour, such as kindness and caring for those in need, your children are more likely to follow in your footsteps. Remember, much of what you teach your children is taught indirectly through what you say and do every day.

As children grow, they will start to encounter new social situations at school and in the community. Your communications towards friends, neighbours, and others you interact with each day will show them how to interact with peers. They will learn how to form healthy friendships and how to navigate difficult situations. Knowing your family's values and staying true to them will help your children embrace them and follow suit as they grow.

Families Provide Protection

Children are not equipped to manage life on their own. After all, children cannot earn income and provide for their own economic security. They need a stable home and strong parents who are committed to their well-being. Children need to feel safe and protected to engage in a healthy way with the world.

When children feel protected, they can enjoy the magic and wonder of childhood. They will not need to waste energy worrying about issues that they cannot control and can engage in meaningful play and favourite pastimes. If difficulties do arise, children can trust that their parents will handle those issues as well.

While physical protection is important, do not overlook the importance of family providing emotional protection. You may have concerns about finances, the health of aging family members, or the stability of your employment.

These are common concerns for adults, but it is usually best to shield children from unnecessary burdens that they have little or no influence over. By doing so, you give them better odds of being able to shoulder the emotional burdens that are typical for their age—keeping up with homework, making new friends, and so on.

What if a serious issue arises? While it may be necessary to involve them at some point, it should be done in a way that is age-appropriate, and only after you have discussed the issue with your partner, spouse, or other adults. Make sure such conversations are not able to be overheard by children. Then, when it is time to discuss the concern with them, limit the details to those that are appropriate, while answering their questions honestly. In doing so, you will help your children feel secure and loved.

When serious difficulties arise, seek support from trusted friends and family to ensure you have enough time for self-care and reflection. Taking care of yourself is key to ensuring that you can be a sensitive and loving parent when your children need you most.

Healthy Families Provide Guidance in All Areas of Life

Families can be a source of support in good times and in bad times. When kids are young, parents can provide advice on playground or friendship issues. As children grow, parents can help them navigate school, sports, activities, and a complex web of relationships.

Parental guidance can extend to helping young people choose universities and careers. For many people, family members are present at major milestones from engagements, to purchasing first homes, to the birth of children. When hardships arise, family can help people traverse difficult passages and build resilience.

It is critical, however, to be mindful and considerate of your child's needs and wants when it comes to offering guidance. In some cases, offering too much support or unwanted guidance can be harmful to family relationships. In general, as children grow and mature, parents should seek to take a mentoring role in their children's lives, offering support in a more Socratic, indirect way, rather than simply telling them what to do or doing it for them.

111

Building Strong Families

Adults need to take the lead in building strong values. Although parents can face pressures from work and community, prioritising family is essential. As children grow, they will have extracurricular activities and friendships that consume much of their time. Never lose sight of the importance of family, even when life gets complicated and busy.

One way to help encourage this is to establish some family traditions that involve dinner together. For example, designating Friday as a pizza and movie night or having a Sunday dinner with extended family are both great ways to accomplish this goal. Some families select a day during the week when family members forgo outside activities and spend the evening at home. During these evenings, families can enjoy dinner, games, crafts, and other enjoyable pastimes.

No matter how busy your family gets, taking time out to talk with each other is important. Start the tradition when kids are young by having one-on-one conversations with each child. Finding time for one-on-one bonding can get more complicated in a larger family. But if you remain flexible and dedicated to the idea, you can make sure everyone in the family feels connected and has their voice heard. Simple traditions like these help give your family a sense of identity.

One thing that can help you identify and create meaningful family traditions is to involve your children in the process. That could include letting your children plan some family activities. It could also mean taking time as a family to decide which traditions you want to continue and which you want to let go of. The importance of family follows each of us through every chapter of life.

Building a strong home and family requires commitment. Parents must dedicate themselves to being present for children and spending time with them. This can be hard when juggling careers and the many complexities of adulthood but every minute that parents spend engaging in positive and meaningful activities with children makes a difference in their lives.

What is your family structure right now?

What value does that structure add to you? In what areas are adjustments needed?

Write the type of family unit that you would like to create or develop; it does not matter what the structure is now, you can recreate something better.

Friendships in Jubilee

This is another key relationship group that must be reviewed as you turn 50. Since it is a time to reset, you might as well reset your friendships. Someone says friends are like elevators—they either take you up or bring you down. And whether we believe it or not, those around us they affect our thinking, behaviours, characters, and desires. Therefore, you must examine those who are around you and make sure you are in a friendship where both parties are adding value to each other.

I am one who has always prided myself in my ability to make friends and relate with people freely. The philosopher, Aristotle said, "In poverty and other misfortunes of life, true friends are sure refuge. They keep the young out of mischief, they comfort and aid the old in their weakness, and they incite those in the prime of life to noble deeds." When I was young, my mum always said that your friends are a reflection of you. I did not fully understand it until I realised that I was keeping some unhealthy friendships. Suddenly, I realised I needed to keep more friends and make new ones that reflect my values and convictions, so now I am making a conscious effort to choose my friends wisely.

There are great benefits of friendships when we find the right friends. Are you saying there are wrong friends? Absolutely yes, and I have experienced a few of those. We must recognise that there are four core types of friendships:

- Acquaintances
- Good friends
- Close friends
- Covenant friends

All these types of friendships play different roles and we must not confuse their purposes or their roles. It is important to also know that it is not all friendships that will last forever. Some friendships are seasonal and you need to know when the season of a friendship is over and to let go, not out of bitterness or offence but that you are both probably in a different place in life and that friendship cannot accommodate or influence that new place or new season.

I don't want to go deep into this chapter on friendship as I already wrote a book about it titled, *Before I Call You My Friend*. You can get a copy of it as it will tremendously bless you and give you information and resources to help you understand and navigate friendships properly.

However, I will advise that as you grow older and settle into your later years in life, you need covenant friends—those who have come to accept you fully and unconditionally, those who value what you value, that you share the same convictions with, that are happy with your success in life and push you to go further and higher. They are not threatened by your gifts and potentials, they will defend you behind your back, are willing to sow into your life and invest quality into the friendship. They are those that you can contribute into each other's families positively.

As I turned 50, I had to reassess my values and convictions, my identity, my desires and pursuit and I had to also look at my friendships and see how many of them fit the new me and who can continue this journey of life on a covenant level with me. I still have the other core friendships in my life, but I understand my investment and expectations of those friendships.

You may think the issue of friendships is trivial or it does not matter but I assure you that it is extremely important and I want you—as you read these few pages on friendship—to stop and do some examinations.

1. Do you understand and do you have expectations for this four core friendship types?
2. How has friendship affected your life?
3. What lessons have you learnt from friendships?
4. As your seasons change in life, what type of friends are you looking for? Do you have them in your life already or are you yet to meet them?

Reflection:

Take time to reflect on this chapter and write out your thoughts and instructions from the Lord.

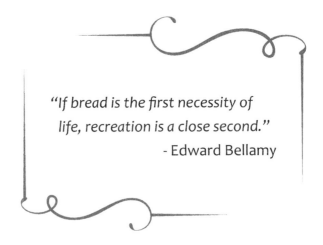

"If bread is the first necessity of life, recreation is a close second."
- Edward Bellamy

Chapter 7

Fun and Recreation in Jubilee

"The bow cannot always stand bent, nor can human frailty subsist without some lawful recreation." – Saavedra

"Recreation and diversion are as necessary to our well-being as the more serious pursuits of life." – Brigham Young

IMPROVING YOUR quality of life is also very key as you journey through life. It is all about balance even though we humans have become too busy and keep getting busier than ever. Finding a way to balance the pressures of work and family with physical and mental wellbeing is important.

We do not need to be told about the value and necessity of work. Yes, work is necessary, and to put bread on the table and a roof over our heads, we admit that we must work. It is one of the first questions we ask our children; what do you want to be when you grow up? And while we do not necessarily expect them to have an answer—or end up doing what they say they will—we are already priming them to think about work. On the other hand, play, recreation, and leisure are seen as ancillary—things we could do without if we had to. However, like a lack of play in children, a lack of recreation can have grave consequences for adults.

People who make recreation a priority are more likely to feel satisfied with their lives overall, according to an American Recreation Coalition Study in 2000. In fact, 90 percent of respondents who said they participate in regular, outdoor recreation reported satisfaction with their overall lives. Sometimes we let life get to us so much that we lose a sense of enjoying the journey as we go, we get so engrossed in the hustle and bustle of life that we don't factor fun and enjoyment into our lives.

I remember as a young mum, I was lucky that both my husband and I valued our fun and recreation. We prioritised it as a family and we travelled, went on outings and bonded as we continued to progress in life and as our family continued to grow. One of the things that helped us greatly in making sure we had fun, created time for recreational activities and built power memories for our family was when we lived in the USA for 9 years—Americans as you may already know love life and they live it to the fullest, they don't need a passport to create amazing fun things for the family. That culture encourages very strong family ties more than here in the UK, and even more than we do in the African community.

Aristotle placed great importance on recreation, or as he called it, leisure. In fact, he believed that we needed to have time for leisure in order to be fully human (therefore, those in his society who only worked without time for leisure were to him incapable of being fully alive). While today we may use the term leisure to mean mindlessly vegging out on the couch or tanning on some beach, leisure, for Aristotle, was specifically the engagement in some activity that allowed for human flourishing—the discussion of philosophical concepts, listening to music, the reading of poetry etc. Leisure was not merely the absence of an activity, or even the lack of work, but rather an active posture of receiving and being.

It was then that I began to lay more emphasis on not just fun and recreation as a family but also as my individual self, understanding what I love to do to keep myself excited and enjoy my journey in life. I realised that it is easy to get so caught up with life in being a wife, husband, mummy, daddy, daughter, employee that we don't enjoy our lives, we become so burdened by bills and caring for everyone else that we become lost in the whole process. So, I started to ask myself, what do I really enjoy that I can recreate and have fun with?

Stop here for a moment and ask yourself the same question. What do you love to do to have fun and relax apart from your mummy and your wifely duties?

Taking time off to indulge in what interests us makes us a

119

better person. We all know the importance of the three Rs of leisure—relaxation, recreation and rest. They help us have a positive attitude to life, develop a balanced perspective and make us look at situations in a new way.

Deadlines are always looming, and the clock never seems to stop ticking. So, what can be done in order to balance work and relaxation? Well, the first thing you can do is prioritise tasks. We often end up doing work that is urgent but not important. Keep your focus on the important stuff, once that is out of the way, you can decide what deserves your attention next.

Take up the long-neglected hobby you enjoy. The right pastime can be so absorbing that it takes your mind off work and helps you relax. Aim to experience something new each day. It can be as simple an activity as tasting a new dish or viewing sunset with your friends or even taking a walk alone in the park. Discover your inner self.

I was well in my 40s when I decided to begin to re explore my inner self and discover new hobbies and what I have a passion for in terms of fun and recreation. I discovered I love girls' night out and I try to do this monthly with different groups of friends—some just for socialising while others inspire and challenge me to be better at what I do for others.

I also love the spa so I schedule monthly visits to different spas. Some people might say that it is expensive but my answer will be that I am worth it and there are ways you can get cheaper options e.g. by using vouchers and coupons. When you use these options, you will get affordable fun and recreational activities and I encourage you to go for it.

I found out that many women especially in my generation kind of lost sight of enjoying life the moment they became wives and mothers; they totally neglect themselves at the expense of being the best wife and best mummy. I am a firm believer of a good balance, which means it's ok to be a great wife and a great mother to your children but you must be a great person to yourself and nurture and care for yourself. You must make sure that life does not pass you by, that you are enjoying it to the fullest and it's overflowing to others.

Many from our mothers' generation failed at enjoying their lives, they sacrificed all for being wives and mothers that the moment the children left home, their lives stopped. They had lost touch with what they loved to do, they stopped developing and exploring their inner selves because of wife and mummy duties. I see many in my age bracket now at the risk of ending up like many of our mothers, hence why I am asking you now to take care of yourselves. It is possible to be a great mum, a great wife and still enjoy other aspects of life that makes life rich and whole.

Get a holistic plan for your life that includes fun and recreation, take up new interests and adventure.

Here are some benefits of having some great fun and recreation as part of your life:

- Reduces stress
- Boosts your self esteem
- Rejuvenates your inner self

- Makes you feel more youthful and energetic
- Improves your relationships

Life is too short to just exist and give up once your season changes, make sure as you are growing now, you plan to not just survive in life but to thrive in life.

Now go ahead and reflect on this chapter and begin to intentionally look at how to spice up your life.

"The things you do for yourself are gone when you are gone, but the things you do for others remain as your legacy""

\- Kalu Ndukwe

Chapter 8

Finally, Your Legacy

"The purpose of life is not to be happy. It is to be useful, to be honourable, to be compassionate, to have it make some difference that you have lived and lived well." – Ralph Waldo Emerson

AFTER ALL is said and done, after all your hustle and bustle, what will you be remembered for? How will you finish? What will you finish with? What will those coming behind you take from you and continue? The bible says a good man leaves an inheritance for his children's children. I don't believe this inheritance should only be money or brick and mortar but it should be something life changing and transforming that another generation can continue in.

By 50, you must fully cross over from the rat race of life into your God-given race of life and begin the journey of creating a lasting legacy for your children's children, something you will build for God that your children will partake of.

Let's take for example some of those I believe have built a legacy, these are my heroes—people like Kenneth Copeland, Pat Robertson of CBS, Billy Graham and my former mentor, Dr Myles Monroe. These are men who built a legacy that whenever the Lord calls them home, they are still living and impacting another generation.

Are you building anything for God? What is the totality of your life right now? One of the strange bewilderments of life is that so many entirely competent leaders finish their leadership journey without leaving behind much of a trace, while others—not necessarily more brilliant—leave behind a legacy.

A legacy should be deeply considered. It takes on immortality, and it is how we live on after death. If we think of our legacy as a gift, it places an emphasis on the thoughtful, meaningful, and intentional aspects of legacy. The consequences of what we do now will outlive us. What we leave behind is the quality of our life, the summation of the choices and actions that we make in this life, our spiritual and moral values.

If you want to leave behind more than a memory; if you genuinely want to change your world and leave a legacy for the long term, you must actively begin to think and plan for what your legacy will be. As a matter of fact, you should start now—no matter what your age is, start preparing to leave a legacy. It is very key and you must prioritise it. Please don't dismiss this because some religious people defer in their legacy building because they believe if they do, they will die early. Many in our fathers' generation believed this myth and they died without a good legacy—we are of a different dispensation so let us be wise.

Stop here for a minute and ask yourself, what do I want to be remembered by? What legacy do I want to build?

If you have not thought about a legacy, it's because of some things happening which you should not allow and I would like to share with you some legacy blockers. These blockers are very dangerous because they keep you pouring out energy on things that won't last and totally distract you from what matters the most.

- **Lack of Focus**

  Losing focus is so subtle because life can get so busy and be so overwhelming depending on the season you are in, so much can be happening at the same time or one after another that if you don't stop and grab yourself, you can be totally lost in the hustle pool of life. You can be so lost in trying to make so many ends meet that you are totally out of focus on not just what matters but what will matter when you cross over.

  Sometimes the enemy plans it for us to lose focus to begin to major on minor and minor on major. I believe coming into the jubilee season of life requires you to have excused some things out of your life and you are living a purpose-filled life rather than just existing and trying to balance.

If you have your hands in too many things, you are bound to lose your focus. If the cares of this world has engulfed you fully, you will lose focus. There has to be a time in the journey of life that you let go of some things and begin to embrace other significant things. There are certain things that become unnecessary as you grow in age and other things that becomes necessary for you to engage in.

- **Living the Life Others Want You to Live**
  Living life the way others want you to live only leads to a life of frustration and regrets. God is the master planner of your life. We all go through a season in life where what others say or do have a huge effect on our lives. In those building years where you want to make the most financially, you begin to ask what the most lucrative career or business venture to go into is. Many of us have ventured into things that if God had not had mercy on us to redirect our steps when we got stuck and sought him for answers, we many never have had the opportunity to build.

  What one leaves behind is the quality of one's life, the summation of the choices and actions one makes in this life, our spiritual and moral values. Legacy starts at the point of discovering your purpose in God—that is what gives you the path to follow and the foundation of what you are going to build that will outlive you. You cannot follow the Jones all your life, you cannot live a fulfilling life by doing what others think you should do, at some point you must stop and ask yourself and God what your life is all about. Many have wasted years pursuing a dead-end and if care is not taken, it may be too late. I pray it will not be late for any of us in Jesus name.

Legacy blockers:
- Lack of focus.
- Living the life others want you to live.
- Bitterness, anger, and fear.
- Consumerism.
- Urgencies that smother priorities.
- Safety.
- Defeatism (It won't matter).

Build your legacy by eliminating behaviours and attitudes that dilute impact. It is not enough to add only positive behaviours, you also need to eliminate the bad.

Ten Ways to Build a Powerful Legacy:
- Dare to be joyful: Serve in ways that bring you joy. Angry, unhappy people leave sad legacies.
- Monitor your impact on others: What are you doing when you make the biggest difference? Do more of that.
- Develop and maximise your talent, strengths, and skills.

- Do what matters now. Everyone who is at the end of life says it goes by fast.
- Seize small opportunities, big ones may follow. Stop waiting to make a difference.
- Start with those closest to you and the ones you spend the most time with.
- Bring your best self to work and family. Everyone has at least two selves. Bring out the best one.
- Think service not success.
- Relax. Don't run around building a legacy. Run around making a difference.
- Elevate the needs of others over your own.

"No one is useless in this world who lightens the burdens of another."

– Charles Dickens

1. **Know What Matters**

   You cannot leave behind a legacy by accident (well, you can, but it's usually a negative one). Until you know, clearly and unambiguously, what you want your legacy to be, it's tough, if not impossible, to begin building it.

   The foundation of building a legacy is a deep sense of *knowing*—not just knowing what is important to you, but what is *non-negotiable*. In a sense, it does not matter what those non-negotiables are. They could revolve around corporate culture, team building, production quality, customer service, innovation, or any one of a thousand other things. What matters is that *you* know what they are. It helps to put your non-negotiables down on paper. Write a manifesto. Print off a pdf and paste it in places where you can easily see it. Revise it regularly, over time, amending the words to clarify and hone your non-negotiables. Strip away everything that is merely a "nice to have", until the manifesto sings your legacy a cappella—clearly and uncluttered by distracting background melodies.

2. **Get Off the Front Line**

Take a look at your list of non-negotiables. It will not take root in your organisation (and you can't build your legacy) if you're stuck permanently in the weeds of managing the day to day details of your business, division, department, project, group or team.

Yes, managers leave legacies too, but they are different. Manager legacies are tactical, anecdotal, of the "do you remember so-and-so?" sort. We are talking about leaving a leadership legacy—a touchstone to guide future generations. That cannot be built from behind a spreadsheet or in the bowels of a PowerPoint deck. Find a COO. Delegate more. Redraw your job description. Make Fridays a "no-managing" day.

However you manage it, if you're serious about leaving a leadership legacy, you need to get out of the front line and spend time—lots of time—with people.

3. **Nauseate yourself**

What do you do with your people now that you've stepped away (at least somewhat) from the front line? Answer: Make yourself ill.

Seems strange right? Well, here is the thing, if you spend time with truly great leaders, leaders who are building a lasting legacy, you'll notice they all have one thing in common. They repeat their non-negotiables endlessly. They do so verbally and by example. They do it in meetings, both formal and informal; they repeat them in one-on-ones; in performance reviews and all-staff meetings; in writing and on the phone; they regurgitate them as the answer to as many questions as tortured logic will allow. They recycle them, reprint them, reinforce them, insistently. Great leaders drive home their non-negotiables over and over again, to the point where they feel physically ill at the thought of repeating them even one more time.

One industry leader I've worked with for over 20 years told me that he only began to drive his personal leadership vision into his company after twelve years of ceaseless pounding on his "non-negotiables".

When the sound of your own voice repeating the same basic principles one more time makes you feel sick, *then* you have started the construction of your legacy.

4. **Leave**

Leaving a legacy behind requires you to no longer be there. Sadly, many leaders miss this vital point, and hang around too long, lingering until the point when what would have been a towering legacy is diminished with time. This happens not just in business. It happens regularly in sports, religion, politics, and entertainment too. Think of how many well-known leaders in their field would have left a much more substantial legacy had they simply stepped away earlier.

Do yourself—and your legacy—a favour. Quit while you are at the top. Go transform some other parts of your life.